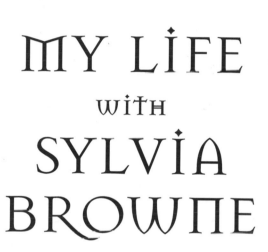

MY LIFE

with

SYLVIA
BROWNE

OTHER HAY HOUSE TITLES OF RELATED INTEREST

By Sylvia Browne:

Books

Adventures of a Psychic (with Antoinette May)

Astrology Though a Psychic's Eyes
(available November 2000)

Conversations with the Other Side
(available November 2000)

God, Creation, and Tools for Life (available March 2000)

Meditations (available November 2000)

The Nature of Good and Evil (available November 2000)

The Other Side and Back (with Lindsay Harrison)*

Soul's Perfection (available June 2000)

Audios

Angels and Spirit Guides

Healing the Body, Mind, and Soul

Making Contact with the Other Side

The Other Side of Life

Sylvia Browne's Tools for Life (available April 2000)

*Not available through Hay House

By Other Authors:

Books

Born to Be Together: *Love Relationships, Astrology, and the Soul,* by Terry Lamb

The Contact Has Begun: *The True Story of a Journalist's Encounter with Alien Beings,* by Phillip H. Krapf
(also available as an audio book)

Developing Your Intuition with Magic Mirrors
(book and card pack), by Uma Reed

Healing with the Angels*,* by Doreen Virtue, Ph.D.
(also available as an audio)

Indigo Children: *The New Kids Have Arrived,*
by Lee Carroll and Jan Tober

Millennium 2000, by Louise L. Hay and Friends

Audios

Messages of the Celestine Prophecy, by Salle and James Redfield, with Michael Toms

Mystical Power, by Marianne Williamson

Psychic and Intuitive Healing, by Barbara Brennan, Rosalyn Bruyere, and Judith Orloff, M.D., with Michael Toms

The above titles are available at your local bookstore, or may be ordered by calling Hay House at 800-654-5126

Please visit the Hay House Website at: **www.hayhouse.com**

MY LIFE
WITH
SYLVIA
BROWNE

A Son Reflects on Life
with His Psychic Mother

CHRIS DUFRESNE

Hay House, Inc.
Carlsbad, California • Sydney, Australia

Published and distributed in the United States by:
Hay House, Inc., P.O. Box 5100, Carlsbad, CA 92018-5100
(800) 654-5126 • (800) 650-5115 (fax)

Editorial: Jill Kramer   *Design:* Jenny Richards
Interior Photos: Larry Beck

Library of Congress Cataloging-in-Publication Data

Dufresne, Chris.
     My life with Sylvia Browne　:　a son reflects on life with his psychic mother / Chris Dufresne.
        p.   cm.
     ISBN 1-56170-667-1 (trade paper)
     1. Browne, Sylvia.   2. Psychics—United States—Biography.
I. Title.
BF1027.B76.D84   2000
133'.092—dc21
[B]   99-44831
                                   CIP

ISBN 1-56170-667-1

02 01 00 99   4 3 2 1
First Printing, December 1999

Printed in the United States of America

DEDICATION

To my most precious gifts from God—my exquisite daughter, Angelia; my joyful boy, William; and my ever-patient wife Gina.

ACKNOWLEDGMENT

To my mother, Sylvia Browne, without whom this book would not have been possible.

CHAPTER ONE

I suppose you've surmised by now that my name is Christopher Dufresne. I am a psychic, and my mother is the famous clairvoyant Sylvia Browne. My hope is that you truly enjoy reading all that I have to tell you—and that you can flow with the informal stream-of-consciousness style that this book is written in. Sometimes I'll mix a little bit of this with a little bit of that—but all in all, I think you'll find my family's story quite entertaining!

Beginnings

My mother and I come from a long line of psychics. For some reason, in a psychic family the gift of clairvoyance is usually relegated to the females. But my great-uncle, Paul Coil, was a psychic; and my great-great-uncle, Henry Kaufholz, was also a spiritualist and psychic. My predecessors tended to keep a low profile—until my mother came along. She's a breed apart, personifying psychic ability in the public eye. Good for her, I say, but that's not *my* style. When I was younger, I appeared on *Evening Magazine, Pacific Currents, Super Kids, Bay City Limits,* and *People Are Talking.* I had a small part in *Unsolved Mysteries,* and

I've also appeared on two episodes of *The Montel Williams Show*. However, my preference is to remain in the background.

I am 33. I have a beautiful wife, Gina; a psychic six-year-old daughter, Angelia (who inherited the love of the spotlight from her grandmother), and a precious baby boy, William. Despite all of this esoteria whizzing around, I think of us as a normal family. Let's face it, if it's all you've known and grown up with, your definition of "normal" can get a bit blurred.

My earliest recollection of being different is when I was around three years old, which seems to be the optimum age for an inherent psychic gift to start showing up. I began to have very clear visions of what I now know was a life before this one. I told my mother in great detail about living a life in the Old West. I vividly remembered being shot outside a saloon, with my horse, Cinder, standing close beside me. As I lay in the dirt, my daughter ran out and held my head in her lap while my soul went out of my body and into the tunnel. My mother listened very attentively and asked questions at the appropriate times, without ever coaching me or leading me on. She said later that it wasn't just the specifics that impressed her, but the fact that I talked about a "daughter"—not a concept a three-year-old boy is likely to concoct.

Like my mother, I knew at a very young age who was sick—sometimes before they even knew it themselves—and I could tell who was at the door or on the phone before anyone had answered. I gave my friends a lot of advice, disguising it as opinions as best I could without tipping them off that I was really giving them psychic insights.

By the time I started school, my mother had been on the local TV program *People Are Talking* for ten years and was very well known in Northern California. That didn't make school a nightmare, but it wasn't exactly a nonstop picnic either—I squared off at least three times with a boy who made some stupid remark about my mother. For the most part, though, especially when I started appearing on a few local TV shows myself, I was treated with a kind of cautious respect.

I have to add here that I've always had a relatively hot temper, and when I was younger, I *did* enjoy a good fight. That's another thing I owe to my predecessors—there's a definite belief in respect and propriety and love and protection in my family. In fact, my mother and I have often joked that, with *her* temper, if she were a male she'd be dead by now.

My beloved grandfather, who passed away four years ago, used to love telling a story about me when I was an infant. My mother was driving, with me right beside her, when a guy ran a light and almost hit us. My mother flew out of our car, screaming, "You could have killed us!" and proceeded to kick her pointed-toed shoe right through his door.

I should mention, with honest humility, that I can read my mother better than she can read herself. But psychics can't read *themselves*. We get vague forebodings and anxieties, but we just don't know where to put them.

My mother's mentor was her grandmother, Ada Coil, whom she adored. And just as my mother had Grandma Ada, I've had my mother, who has not only enhanced my confidence throughout my life about my psychic gift, but has also inspired me to keep going, reminding me of all the good we do and the enormous joy we often share with others.

I was never trained to be a psychic. I'm convinced that you can't be formally trained for this, although you can certainly learn to hone your intuition to a greater extent. My mother was always around to offer encouragement and support, and very early in my 17 years of readings, I realized the truth of what she's always said: "No one but you and God are in that reading room."

The Psychic Gift

As far back as I can remember, our house was always filled with people. They stood outside when it was warm, and they hung out in the laundry room when it was cold—all of them waiting to see Mom for a reading. With nothing else to compare it to, I assumed ours was a normal household. Didn't every mother "know" things? Didn't all moms have people lining up to see them? I was genuinely surprised when I found out somewhere along the line that this wasn't considered normal at all.

My mom treated my psychic gift and its countless ramifications as a matter of fact, as had her grandmother when Mom was a child, and it created a great closeness between us. I thought nothing of my mother holding classes in our house every Tuesday, and trances every Friday. My brother, Paul, on the other hand, although he loved our mother, seemed to be embarrassed by the whole thing. He was conspicuously absent during family trances when my mom's spirit guide, Francine, would take over and "speak" to us and our friends. He confided in me once that it frightened him. Whether he was afraid that when Mom tranced she wouldn't come back or he just didn't like the whole idea, I'm not sure. I just know that, for whatever reason, Paul was spooked.

But scared or not, I had no choice. I had this gift, and what's more, I *knew* I had it. Like my mom, I was also compelled to test it. I would receive information and then set out to prove or disprove it. I have to admit, when I was younger, I would almost hope I was wrong, like when I "saw" a friend roll his truck—but no such luck. Trying to warn my friends never worked, and that could be very discouraging.

I guess Mom was right—"A prophet in their own land is always a stranger."

My brother was a far more mild-mannered child than I was. Looking back, I'm convinced that psychic ability doesn't sit as easily in the male mind as in the female mind because it comes in on the emotional side. So, temperamental, tough, and competitive as I am, it still sits hard sometimes.

I loved sports and still do. I made Athlete of the Year in grade school and say that without humility, because I worked damned hard for it. I ran the Bruce Jenner Classic race, and I loved wrestling in high school. I was also courted by coaches and scouts for my ability as a soccer player, much to Mom's dismay. Although she didn't say so at the time, she was afraid it would interfere with my chart. She knew that I would follow her some-day, just as I know my daughter, Angelia, will receive the scepter from *me* someday . . . and the beat goes on.

Some Basic Terms

Before I really get started, perhaps I should take a moment to explain some basic terms that my family uses. If you are familiar with my mother's work, then you already know that almost everyone has a *spirit guide.* Truly evil sociopathic individuals don't have them, according to Mom, but since those people never come to us for readings, we haven't had to confront a client without their spirit guide right there with them.

A spirit guide is an entity who's assigned to you on the *Other Side,* which is where most souls go after physical life ceases. These entities have been trained intensively to help you during any given life on Earth. Spirit guides direct us, know and have memorized our charts, and can help us out of any number of dangerous situations if we'll only listen. They can be male or female, and I've found that they seem to complement our personalities or essences. My mother's guide, Francine, for example, is a very serious, no-nonsense woman—not at all the often hilarious personality Mom can be. My guide, Charlie, is fairly laid back, positive, and fun-loving. Not that I don't love a good time as much as anyone, but I tend to be more serious, analytical, and intense, so Charlie and I are a good combination.

Please don't misunderstand anything by looking at Mom's and my situations—it's just as common for women to have male guides and for men to have female guides. We recruit our guides on the Other Side based on the compatibility of their essences and ours, and gender is too trivial to even take into consideration.

Our spirit guides are with us long before we enter a body for another lifetime, and they're among the first to greet us when we return Home to the Other Side again. They have lived at least one lifetime on Earth, so they understand what it's like to occupy a body and experience the joys and pitfalls of being human. As such, they can offer advice and guidance with a healthy dose of empathy. And since they have studied our charts and know them better than we do on a conscious level, a good analogy is that while we're the ones driving the "car" of our life, they're the ones sitting beside us holding the map.

Most of us will go through extensive spirit-guide training when we're on the Other Side so that we're able to provide guidance to others in the same loving way that our own loving guides did with us.

When I was five, I was very aware of being able to summon my little imaginary friends. Later, of course, I realized that they were not imaginary at all, but *earthbounds* who came around me because they knew I could see them. Earthbounds are souls who, after death, do not make the transition to the Other Side for some reason, but remain on the Earth plane as what are commonly called spirits, haunts, or ghosts. One in particular was named Joey, and he looked badly scarred, as if he had been in a fire. He would pull my spirit out at night for astral travel, and we would go and play on the steps of a beautiful Romanesque-looking building. Francine, my mother's spirit guide, told her that a little earthbound and I had been playing on the steps of the *Hall of*

Wisdom, where all souls go after their souls have left their physical bodies and passed through the tunnel.

When our bodies die and our spirits go through the tunnel to the Other Side, we're taken first to the Hall of Wisdom by our spirit guides and our angels to review the lives we've just lived. We assess our lives and decide what we did right and what we did wrong, and it's then up to us whether we want to make our corrections on the Other Side or come back in another incarnation to improve on the success of our soul's mission toward perfection.

Angels are pure entities, which simply means spirit entities who never incarnate and become flesh. They are God's warriors, companions, messengers, and protectors, who come to Earth with us and our guides to help us throughout our lives. Their skin, hair, and eye colors can vary, but their features are invariably perfect, androgynous, and very, very beautiful.

Apparently my mother didn't mind my being out after my bedtime, as long as I only did it astrally, but she was concerned about Joey, who, as an earthbound, didn't know he was dead. By being his friend, I was keeping him nearby and not allowing him to go on. Mother and I had a long talk about my letting Joey go, and I threw a huge fit about it. I didn't want to lose my friend. But after what seemed like weeks of her explaining that Joey had to go to his family and that I was being selfish, I finally had a tearful talk with him about it, during which time I made him a promise I fully intend to keep—we *will* see each other again.

I shouldn't continue any further without telling you about Charlie. He is my spirit guide, just as Francine is my mother's. Unlike my mother, though, I don't channel my spirit guide through trance, nor do I ever plan to. I remember once when Mom was in a trance, I began to feel a whirling darkness enveloping me, and with a resounding "No!" I pushed the feeling away.

Maybe it's because males like to be more in control. Or maybe it's just because *I* do.

I do feel my guide's strong presence and get very clear mental messages from him. I don't have actual auditory contact with Charlie, but after seeing the aggravation Mom goes through with what she calls her "chirping guide," I'm almost relieved. She and I both have the same idiosyncrasy of talking to our guides while we're taking a shower (spirits often use water as a convenient form of transportation from their dimension to ours), somehow believing that no one else can hear us. Not so. The family was just too polite to bring it up to our faces.

My brother, Paul, by the way, like my mother's sister, Sharon, is not psychic, nor are any of my cousins. Genetically, the psychic gift is definitely a real hit-or-miss kind of thing.

From the time I was in kindergarten through about the fourth grade, I could *astrally project* at will. I remember sitting with my mother on the couch one day, asking her to watch what I could do, and then I promptly exited my body. She told me later that from her point of view, I slumped, and suddenly she heard muted running and saw my small, distinct footprints making circles around her in the freshly vacuumed rug. I can still hear her ordering, "Chris, get in here and stay in here!"

She then asked if I was leaving my body like that during math class. It seems that my teacher had told her I appeared to go to sleep every day at math time and wake up again the minute class was over. Not given to lying, especially to Mom, I told her that yes, I was, because I thought math was boring and I would much rather be with my friends. She gave me a few firm ground rules about the timing on my astral trips, and I actually began to excel at math. In fact, to this day, it's one of my best subjects.

Astral projection is a phenomenon that my daughter, Angelia (who has renamed herself Eya) and I are more proficient at than Mom is. She's done it a few times, but she feels she's busy enough with her voices, visions, and spirits without consciously leaving her body from time to time. She does "step aside" when she trances, of course, to allow Francine to use her eyes, ears, and voice to communicate with others, and she so completely "vacates" for Francine that she has no memory of what takes place while her spirit guide is in charge.

Eya (I will interchange the names Angelia and Eya through-out the book) astrally projects fairly often, and I did it more fre-quently when I was younger than I do now, but anyone can do it with practice—it's simply the process of the soul, which is the true essence of who we are, temporarily leaving the body, which is nothing more than the vehicle we inhabit while we're on Earth. As Mom points out on this subject, astral projection is just more proof that the soul is its own separate and eternal entity. It's been dis-cussed for centuries, and before people understood what was hap-pening, the astral projectionists were frankly thought to be crazy.

When your soul leaves your body to astrally project, it may simply stay nearby, and you could easily start with the experience of hovering near the ceiling looking down at yourself. People going through surgery have frequently documented viewing themselves and the entire operation while under full general anes-thesia, being able to repeat word-for-word what was said and move-for-move what happened even though they were supposed-ly "out cold."

Even when it occurs during surgery, astral projection is not a near-death experience. There's no tunnel and no reason to be afraid. It usually starts with a buzzing sensation in the head, fol-lowed by a vibration, a feeling of wind rushing by, and if you don't panic at this point, the soul—often with a loud pop—will exit the body. Some astral projectionists are convinced that the soul exits and reenters through the top of the head. I've never been that specific about it. I just feel a "lift-off" and I'm "out."

If you decide to try it, I can't stress enough to ask God to keep the white light of the Holy Spirit around you to protect you, ask for a fast exit and reentrance, and rather than just hanging around your bedroom during the experience, you might ask to go someplace specific. Knowing where you're going during astral travel is important and can make you feel more in control of the "trip." Ask to visit deceased loved ones, or to explore the Other Side to verify what you've heard or read about the geography, structures, and so on.

Dreams of flying are definitely astral projections during sleep—your soul really is soaring above mountains and oceans and among the stars. And you know that feeling of virtual paralysis you sometimes wake up with, especially after one of those "dreams"? That's simply caused by the suddenness of being awakened, and your soul being caught off guard and finding itself momentarily half in and half out of your body. But astral travel, with the infinite experiences it makes possible, is very exhilarating and rejuvenating. According to Francine, Mom's spirit guide, we all astrally travel and check in with Home on the Other Side at least three times every month or so—we just don't necessarily remember.

Life Charts and Themes

On the Other Side, before we come to Earth, we diligently research what we want to learn, how we will learn it, and even where we can go to meet those goals. Based on that research, we write the charts that form the road maps for the lives we're about to live. It's not unlike picking a college and then specifically choosing our course of study. In the process of composing our charts, we're advised by a group of Master Teachers and another group called the Council, and we also confer with the spirit guides we've chosen to help us fulfill those charts.

We choose the pitfalls we'll face, the highs and the lows, and we define the situations we'll place ourselves in from the beginning of this lifetime to the end. We devise and review and rewrite and review our charts again and again before we start each lifetime to make sure we'll be satisfying our determination to continue growing in our spirituality for God. In these charts, we build in purposes or themes to work on, conquer, and ultimately perfect, so that each of us really is here for a very definite reason. Everyone is born with primary and secondary life themes. They're what we come into life to perfect—in effect, they serve as our purpose for living.

When Mom and I do readings, what we're really "reading" is the chart of the client we're with, including the themes and purposes they've written in. That's part of the value of a reading—to help the client understand why they're here and what lessons, both large and small, they're here to learn.

For example, I just did a reading a few days ago in which I said to a woman, "You know, you came into this life with a rejection theme." She screamed and said, "That explains why I suffer so much at even the slightest rebuff!" Once a theme has been pointed out for exactly what it is, we can often break its hold on us and go on. Mind you, everyone experiences rejection in their lifetime, but it only affects you on the deepest soul level if it's your theme.

We all choose two themes to write into our charts—one primary and the other secondary. The primary theme is what we are or what we're here to accomplish, while the secondary theme is what we have to overcome along the way. Once in a while, a brave soul will take on both a negative primary theme and a negative secondary theme—Rejection and Victim, for example (see the list on the next page), but there is something to be gained in every theme, no matter how negative it might appear to be.

There are 45 themes that we choose from, and there are so many last-lifers around these days that it's hard for them to recognize their two themes immediately because they've had so many lives that they find they can relate to all 45 themes. This doesn't mean we have to go through all 45 before we're finished experiencing life on Earth. Again, just like in school, we pick and choose what we feel our souls need to perfect.

I need to remind you that not for a moment should we leave God out of this, or out of *anything,* for that matter. Above and beyond the Master Teachers, the Council, and our spirit guides, it's God who helps us the most to compose our charts and make our choices for the advancement of our souls. Our relationship with God is truly a partnership, similar to that of a parent and child.

Mom has gone into great detail about the 45 life themes in her book *Adventures of a Psychic.* They've been compiled by her and her fellow hypnotists through literally thousands of regressive past-life sessions and other exhaustive research. I'll simply list the themes here and encourage you to turn to her wonderful book for a more thorough discussion of this subject.

THE 45 LIFE THEMES

ACTIVATOR—feels driven to get any and all projects completed

AESTHETIC PURSUITS—the person with this theme has a need to create (art, music, etc.), which manifests itself at a young age and dominates the individual's entire life

ANALYZER—has to pull apart and examine everything that is seen, read, or heard

BANNER CARRIER—constantly fighting injustice; this person is on God's picket line of enforcers

BUILDER—the silent one who helps others achieve their goals

CATALYST—the "Alka Seltzer" added to the water of life to make things happen

CAUSE FIGHTER—more than the banner carrier, this person activates to make the world better

CONTROLLER—takes charge and insists that things be done their way

EMOTIONALITY—a hard theme, because this person feels every nuance of energy, hurt, and pain

EXPERIENCER—compelled to taste, see, feel, and experience everything that crosses their path

FALLIBILITY—the person with this theme is a great spirit who has chosen some physical challenge to take on for God's knowledge

FOLLOWER—the shaft without which no arrow could hit its mark

HARMONY—the person with this theme wants every person and every situation to be happy

HEALER—a passion for caring for and curing everyone in their lives

HUMANITARIAN—here to shepherd God's flock with help from His strength

INFALLIBILITY—this person "has it all"—a surprisingly difficult theme to overcome

INTELLECTUALITY—an insatiable search for knowledge, sometimes for its own sake

IRRITANT—the whiner; the doomsday pessimist

JUSTICE—this person fights for an atmosphere of fair play, honesty, and righteousness

LAWFULNESS—this theme involves the pursuit of learning, and strictly upholding the laws of society and morality

LEADER—the take-charge person, usually with an ultimate vision in mind

LONER—a person with an innate need to be quiet and meditative

LOSER—these individuals put themselves in situations in which they're doomed to fail

MANIPULATOR—doesn't just control people, but usually coerces them into liking it in the process

PASSIVITY—the person with this theme can't confront anything or take a stand that might result in any form of dissension

PATIENCE—those with this theme are able to adapt easily to all of life's delays

PAWN—the person who stands between two factions and offers him- or herself as an option

PEACEMAKER—aggressive in the face of all offenders to restore order

PERFORMER—whether in the entertainment field or not, this person is always "on"

PERSECUTION—the person with this theme feels that no matter what happens, it is bad and specifically meant for him or her

PERSECUTOR—the seeming "bad seed" that has a self-chosen role to play that enables humankind to evolve toward perfection

POVERTY—the individual with this theme is perpetually deprived, however much or little one has

PSYCHIC—has the power to see beyond the norm (neither Mom's theme nor mine, by the way)

REJECTION—in a constant state of feeling unloved, hated, and abandoned

RESCUER—compelled to try to save anyone and everyone

RESPONSIBILITY—the person with this theme is a volunteer, hands always raised to take on every task

SPIRITUALITY—the individual with this theme is searching for the truest path

SURVIVAL—doggedly willing to go through the ritual of a so-called humdrum life

TEMPERANCE—locked in a perpetual battle against their tendency toward addiction

TOLERANCE—able to get along with every person and every seemingly impossible situation

VICTIM—here to demonstrate to others the consequences of hard times and bad choices

VICTIMIZER—loves to inflict harm upon others to maintain a sense of superiority

WARRIOR—the risk taker, unusually not afraid of anything

WEALTH—the person with this theme is obsessed with acquiring and hoarding wealth—when this theme is overcome, the individual often gives away wealth freely

WINNER—insists on being the best—in games, business, relationships, and life in general

Our Psychic Family Tree

Unlike most family trees, I'll present ours in reverse order, from today back, focusing on my mother's side of the family. Every ancestor on this list is or was a validated psychic in their time, and was born in the year noted:

> 1992 Angelia Dufresne (who renamed herself Eya), *daughter of Christopher* (the author of this book)
>
> 1966 Christopher Dufresne, *son of Sylvia*

1936	Sylvia Celeste Shoemaker Browne, *mother of Christopher Dufresne*
1904	Paul E. Coil, *son of Ada C. Coil*
1865	Ada C. Coil, *grandmother of Sylvia Browne*
1860	Henry Kaulfholz, *brother of Ada Coil*
1830	Katrina Kaulfholz, *mother of Ada and Henry Coil*
1800	Anna von Banaca, *mother of Katrina Kaulfholz*
1760	Ida Katrina von Banaca, *mother of Anna von Banaca*
1728	Celestine Hoffine, *mother of Ida von Banaca*
1700	Christine Hoffine, *grandmother of Celestine Hoffine*

Even though they were never practicing psychics, two more family members contributed to the psychic bloodline: Mom's father, William L. Shoemaker, who once astounded a board of psychologists by scoring 98 out of 100 percent on a test of ESP abilities; and his mother, Hattie, Mom's grandmother, who thought nothing of seeing the spirits of those who had died, and assumed everyone else could see them as well.

No psychic in our family, including my mother and me, has

ever had much patience with the esoteric nonsense that a few other psychics, both the real ones and the frauds, seem addicted to. We keep our priorities simple: compassion, truth, and above all, God's will. My mom and I can disagree, and I'm not ashamed to say we've had some rousing fights, after which we quickly make up just as rousingly. But not once have we ever fought about our principles of ethics and spirituality and our passion for knowing and following God's plan.

C H A P T E R   T W O

I don't think it's ever easy having a celebrity as a parent, but it's even tougher being constantly asked, "What does your mother have to say? Who does she think will win that game (or boxing match or horse race or beauty contest)?" Of course, as soon as everyone I knew found out that *I* was also a psychic—suddenly it became, "Chris, what do *you* think?" I'm not sure which made me more uncomfortable.

Mom and I independently come up with the same psychic answers about 90 percent of the time. The terminology may vary, but the results are usually right on the mark. For example, I might say, "You will meet a gardener," while Mom will say, "You will meet a horticulturist." She's always been more given than I am to longer, fancier words, although no one has ever accused either one of us of being an intellectual snob!

Mom has fought against her ability at times, but I'm sure she would agree that I fought harder than she did. It wasn't that I thought being psychic wasn't noble or manly, since there are some damned good male psychics and spiritualists out there. I think I was just trying to hang on to my freedom for as long as possible. Sure, in the deep recesses of my soul, I knew I would succumb to my destiny, but I wasn't going down without a fight, I subconsciously decided.

I say "subconsciously" because I never set out to be wild. I prefer to call it *joie de vivre*—love of life. I was never arrested and never did anything illegal—I just wanted "souped-up" trucks, lifted axles, fights, and dances every Friday night—and, I'm not ashamed to admit, many, many girlfriends.

The good news was that Mom had an open house. My brother and I could always bring anyone and everyone home. Parties and food were abundant at our house even though we lived in a poorer section of town. My mother's philosophy about her sons was always, "At least if you're here, I know what you're doing."

I didn't have fantasies about being a cop or a fireman when I was a child. My mom had been married to one of each—so much for romanticizing those careers. However, I did show an aptitude for architectural design. As a kid, I would keep our foster sister, Mary, up until all hours of the night rearranging a room.

Speaking of Mary, she lived with us for 15 years, as did other children who didn't have a home or had a problem in theirs. Mom took them all in. She and I both have the primary theme of Humanitarian. But her secondary theme is Loner, while mine is Warrior. I think my themes fit better than my mom's because of the life we have chosen to live and how hard it is to fight through it sometimes.

My brother, Paul, always kept to himself, while I was, and still am, out in the open about everything. Because we grew up knowing about spirit guides, angels, earthbounds, and hauntings, we were never plagued with night terrors. I never had them, nor did Paul or Mary. We just took for granted that we were here from the Other Side to live out a life and then go Home.

We were by no means the Brady Bunch. I resented that my mother worked so hard with no help from her husbands, and I vowed then that my wife would not work while our children were small—a promise I've kept to this day. My wife, Gina, is able to stay home and give our children the attention that my mother still wishes she'd been free to give Paul, Mary, and me, even though we never for one moment felt neglected or unloved by her.

Growing up, the one thing Mom asked Paul and me not to do was play football. All other sports were okay, but she knew we would be hurt playing that particular sport. She also drilled into us that sitting around watching sports was a way to avoid getting out and living. We pretended to think she was being silly and overprotective, but Paul and I never did play football, and much to our wives' joy, we are not sports fanatics. To this day we would rather engage in certain athletic activites than just watch.

I've been asked if I missed having a father in my life. The answer is, with nothing to compare it to, I don't know. What I do know is, not having had a father has made me determined to be a great father myself. And thank God I had a spectacular grandfather until I was 29, and a mom who, on top of everything else, could help me with such important issues in my life as truck blocks and upgrading my shock absorbers.

I don't remember living with Mom's first husband, Gary (my biological father). I do remember her second husband, Dal, but he really wasn't a force in my life, and he certainly wasn't a strong father figure. My maternal grandfather took on the father-figure role in my life, and, like my mother, I still feel his loss with a deep, hard grief. He came to all my soccer games, took us on weekend trips, and sometimes even attempted a game of basketball. He was and still is my hero, and I know that he walks with me every step of the way to this very day.

My grandfather and my Mom and me had a phenomenal mutual telepathy—one of us would think it, and the other two would answer or be there. Sometimes it was downright funny. Mom would put out the telepathic call to meet her at a particular place and time, and my grandfather and I would show up, just as surely as if we'd had a phone conversation. We even had a hard time going on separate shopping trips without running right into each other nine times out of ten. More than once my friends witnessed all this, shook their heads, and said, "You people are just too spooky."

I began pulling in all sorts of information at around the age of eight or nine. It was random at first, and usually negative. For example, I knew, as I mentioned, that my friend Billy would roll his truck, or that Johnny was going to fall off a fence. Mom explained that psychic ability usually starts this way because negativity travels faster on this plane, but that doesn't make it easier. I'm sure this is what deters a lot of people from even exploring their own psychic abilities more deeply. They don't realize that once they finally get past the negative, they'll be given some positive information, see past the negativity to the light at the end of the tunnel, be given advice to share that can blunt negativity's sharp edges, or even save a life.

I had a hard time understanding how I could extend a meaningful helping hand, or cure or save someone, if our lives were already charted. Then one day I overheard my mother on the phone saying, "How do you know I wasn't written in your chart to warn you, Hazel?" That gave me great comfort and a whole new sense of commitment and determination to make a genuine difference in as many lives as I can.

Mom wanted us all to go through *regression* at an early age to get rid of all our past-life phobias, or "leftovers," as she put it. Regression is a phenomenon that can happen under hypnosis, where we access our memories of this life in reverse order—going back to our childhoods and then infancies—and then beyond, into the deeply recessed memories of our previous life. If desirable, we can go even further to many past lives until we reach whatever event caused the present-day phobia. For example, if you are afraid of water, then perhaps you drowned in a past life. I went under my first hypnotic regressions at the age of 12. We still have a recording of it—my mother meticulously keeps tapes of everything even remotely related to research. My fate was obviously set even at that age. She asked me what my themes were, I told her, and then she asked what I was going to do with them. The transcript reads, "I came down to help you in your work." So there you have it. At 12, I was already signed, sealed, and delivered to the psychic world, both genetically and by my own handwritten chart.

I had lots of friends, and more than my share of devil-may-care tendencies, but I always came home, where Mom would wait for me with candles lit. One night my friend Rob got his truck stuck in a ditch and came to me for help—not just because we were friends, frankly, but also because I happened to have a winch, or towline. We arrived back at his truck and attached the winch, and I started trying to grind up the steep hill. It was very muddy thanks to an earlier hard rain, and before long I began to slip dangerously, headed for a guaranteed jackknife or crash at the bottom of the hill. I remember the moment of pure fear in the pit of my stomach, and then an equally strong feeling of calm, absolute certainty. I turned to Rob, who was as scared as I had been, and announced, "My mom just lit a candle. We're going to make it." I checked the digital clock on my dashboard, and it was exactly 9:00 P.M. when my wheels suddenly grabbed, and Rob's truck groaned its way out of that muddy ditch.

I was still shaken when Rob and I got back to my house, but I tried to keep my voice calm as I stepped through the door and yelled, "Mom, I'm home!"

She came out of her bedroom and simply looked at me with those knowing eyes of hers, not saying a word.

"What time did you light a candle?" I asked.

"The triple trinity hour," she said. "Nine o'clock."

I admit it, I couldn't resist looking at Rob, who was staring with surprise at both Mom and me, and stating the obvious, "Told you, Rob."

In one of Mom's many efforts at family closeness, we lived for a time next to my grandparents and Aunt Sharon. To put it politely, it just didn't work out. Mom left my dad, and she and Paul and I moved into a tenement. Looking back, by the way, I can see why I had so many ear infections as a kid. We had a pool at that tenement, and I loved it and couldn't stay out of it. The truth is, it was full of algae. Mom, determined to put the brightest face possible on our situation, kept insisting it was full of water lilies.

She said we moved because she got tired of the abuse, underplaying as always the guts I know it took to strike out on her own, a single mom with two young boys on a teacher's salary and a meager part-time income from readings and trances. That's when she decided to take the big gamble and focus solely on her destiny—she quit teaching and started doing readings full-time.

CHAPTER THREE

People continued to file in and out of our tenement, waiting to see my mother. Then she met my stepfather, Dal, who allowed her to open up a storefront office. She had always been busy, but as soon as she opened that office, all hell broke loose in the best possible way.

My grandfather had retired and went to work as Mom's secretary, protector, and business agent. I'd go to the office after school and clean up. A year later, she moved to a two-story office building, had six people on staff, and was conducting study groups four nights a week. I continued going to the new office to clean up and then sat at her desk and did my homework. After her study groups, we'd go out to eat and then head home. This routine quickly became comfortable for me.

My mother came from a generation in which females typically deferred to males. She certainly deferred to *her* father, and I'm sure this explains why she's made some unfavorable choices in husbands and lovers. The good news for me was, she also tended to defer to my brother and me, including building us up as the best things that ever hit this world. Now that I've become a parent, I understand not only how well that works, but also what a great responsibility it places on a child. When someone unconditionally loves you that much, you'll move heaven and earth not to lose that feeling or destroy it.

We grew up in a house without religion but with constant spirituality. We had our guides, our angels, and always, always God. We knew about the white light of the Holy Spirit and the Christ Consciousness. We understood karma with a capital "K": You do bad, you'll get it back. We always knew we had lived before, and we were here to serve and give to others so we could complete God's and our contract and then go Home to the Other Side. Being more of an astral projectionist than anyone else in the family, I know what is over there. I've been there, without having to have a death experience, as my mother did when she was 42.

I inherited my great memory from my mother, but obviously you have to rely on other people to fill in a few of the blanks. For example, both my mother and her doctor, Donald Williams, have told me this story: I was born prematurely and weighed 8 lbs., 7 oz. Some preemie. But when I finally came out after 36 hours (poor Mom!), I turned blue. They brought me to her bed, and she, afraid I was dying, dipped her hand in a pitcher of water on the bedside, placed her hand on my head, and said, "I baptize you Christopher Michael Dufresne." Then, in fear and anguish, she held me tightly to her and cried over and over again, "Chris, please don't leave Mama; please don't leave Mama." I will always believe that between my wanting to stay in the womb and her pleading with me never to leave her, Mom and I were bonded on a deep soul level long before I was born.

Particular Abilities

It is important to note that each of us in this family has a different twist on our genetic psychic ability. I can astrally project and do readings. My mother can see spirits and do readings. My grandmother, I'm told, did readings exclusively by channeling her voices—just like psychic Edgar Cayce. My daughter sees spirits, knows the future, and has kinetic energy, which is the ability to mentally manipulate tangible objects. By the sheer untrained power of her little mind, she can turn TVs and lights off and on, has cemented all the wires in our remote control units, and has also caused a few computer crashes, much to the dismay and expense of the office staff. Mom and I have decided that instead of the genes weakening from one generation to the next, Angelia (Eya) is the culmination of all of us who've preceded her.

When I first clearly recognized this fact about my beautiful daughter, it made me both very happy and very, very sad. The psychic road is wondrous, but so hard and so demanding, and the gift owns you. So all of us, especially Mom and me, have always tried to assure her that she comes by her gifts naturally, that she has our constant unconditional love, support, and understanding, and as best she can she should try not to let her gifts make her afraid—which, unfortunately, is impossible.

One day I had been unusually anxious without knowing why. Then Angelia came home from her first-grade class crying. I held her and said, "Angelia, what's wrong?"

Through her tears she managed, "Daddy, I'm so scared. Something bad is going to happen in the family."

My wife, Gina, has been in this family long enough to take these things seriously, so she gathered Angelia and Willy and kept them with her while I began trying to track down my mother, who was on the road lecturing. I didn't sleep much that night waiting for her to call me back, which she finally did, early that morning. She was in a Canadian hotel room, and I didn't have to be psychic to hear in her voice that something had shaken her up. It seems that a ceiling fan in the bedroom of her suite had been running at high speed while she slept, and one of the blades had flown off and hit her arm. As it happened, her arm was over her face. The paramedic told her that if her arm hadn't been exactly where it was, the blade would have hit her throat instead, and she would certainly have been killed.

The instant the phone call with Mom ended, Angelia was calm again, and so was I. The crisis was over. That's the damnable thing about this gift. It doesn't help any of us one bit. We get telepathic warnings, but that's it. The information we're given is right on the mark for everyone else. But not for us.

This explains why no psychic wins the lottery, and why we have to learn our own lessons the hard way like everyone else. Doctors can't operate on themselves, after all, and chiropractors can't adjust their own backs, and so on and so on. William, my precious almost-two-year-old boy, who's built like a tank, does not show signs of the gift, and I have to say that I'm secretly happy about that. He is full of smiles, isn't at all moody, and loves food and life. He is smart as a whip, but he shows no level of consciousness that plumbs the darkness that his sister, father, and beloved grandmother Sylvia are taken to whether we want to go there or not.

I do want to add, though, that Angelia's incredible gift, like Mom's and mine, also brings her great joy and insights thanks to her innate intimacy with spirituality. She was recently helping my mother select flowers to plant in Mom's front yard, and while scanning all the brilliant colors and varieties, commented almost to herself, "God spent a lot of time on these."

CHAPTER FOUR

A t the age of 33, I have now officially been doing readings for 17 years. I know that's hard to believe at my age. I still have trouble believing it myself. My mother didn't start doing readings until she was 19, so by the time I'm her age, I will have beaten her tenure. And while Mom was a schoolteacher for several years and only able to do readings after hours, this has been an almost full-time profession for me since I was 16.

Mom and I each read in our own distinctive styles, but we do both use the same practical "no BS" approach. We don't believe in curses, fortune telling, crystal balls, or cards. We just let go and let God.

Being male, I admit I had to overcome some resistance to my inevitable destiny as a psychic. After all, I've always been determined to be my own person, and who wanted to follow Mom's act, for God's sake? My brother, Paul, wasn't born with the gift and went his own way, becoming a mortgage broker. I wanted to pursue building and architecture and designing blueprints, which I love. But that was not to be. Your mind plays tricks on you, and vice versa. I would tell myself, "I'll just do readings for a while and then get out." My mother confessed to me again just the other day how hard she fought against it. When her spirit guide, Francine, told her she would speak in front of thousands and thousands of people someday, Mom screamed, "No!" and then promptly threw up.

I think psychics are the one group of people who have to always—tiresomely, at times—audit their own minds. As I mentioned before, I don't trance and don't have auditory contact with my guide, Charlie, but I know when he talks, because it's a unique, quiet feeling, and it just ticker-tapes through my mind and is decidedly different from my own thought patterns. But whether the thoughts are coming from Charlie or from somewhere else, I, like all psychics, live in a world of analyzing and sorting and forever trying to keep our own egos out of the way.

Despite the psychic male ancestors I'd been told about, I once ranted at my mother that the psychic world seemed to be the exclusive province of females. She proceeded to sit me down with a collection of Edgar Cayce's books. He was her hero, and he's now mine. We also have George Anderson and John Edwards; the brilliant Arthur Ford; and my mother's friend, the late great Douglas Johnson. It has made me feel so much better to see that male psychics have made as big a contribution to society as female psychics have, and their inspiration has meant a great deal to me.

Mom won't like my saying this, but, like Cayce, she has gone through more than her share of trials and tribulations in this life. Among the worst was when, out of either ignorance or misguided trust in her second husband, Dal, she signed everything he put in front of her and ended up being bankrupt and defamed. I raged against him, believe me. I tried to keep a lot of it to myself in an effort not to make her life even more difficult, but I knew this man was a taker.

I've had my own crosses to bear, of course, but thank God they weren't so public. Most of them have their roots in fear—even now there is a segment of the public who believes that psychics are in league with the devil. That might not enrage me so much if it weren't such an outrageous contradiction of the truth. I won't speak for all psychics, but in my family we love God and are Gnostic Christians, which means that we follow what our Lord said to a T. It's interesting to note that the King James version of the Bible states, "Never suffer a witch to live." Guess what—King James came up with that because he was afraid of witchcraft. The vast majority of other translations read, "Never suffer a poisoner to live." Well, I'm not a poisoner, I don't know any poisoners, and I'm certainly not related to any poisoners, so I don't have much patience when people try to portray psychics as evil by misquoting the Bible. I really do pray that in Angelia's lifetime, when she fulfills her destiny and becomes, I'm sure, the greatest psychic this family has produced, she'll be justifiably appreciated as a gifted and deeply spiritual handmaiden to society and to God.

This period of time, though, especially because of all the millennium hysteria, really is a dichotomy. I'll defend valid spiritual psychics any day of the week, but I'll fight just as hard against those ridiculous psychic hotlines and the glut of charlatans who have jumped on the psychic bandwagon with no gifts to offer—but more than their share of fast-talking, obscene greed.

My mother's church has two locations and 50 ministers to support. She has a huge staff, and it grows every day. These people have been with her for most of my lifetime and have become our extended family. They have gone through our pregnancies, family deaths, illnesses, heartaches, and the birth of our children, whom they spoil rotten, and we in turn have been there for all of theirs as well. That is the way I believe it's supposed to be—a group of dedicated people who love and help each other. We have no particular dogma, except to do right by God and do good for each other and for humankind. We don't just talk the talk, we really walk the walk.

Unless she's on the case of a missing child, which stays with her constantly until it's solved one way or another, Mom somehow manages to put her readings in a separate place in her mind when they're finished and go back to them again later. I, on the other hand, have to fight to let go of my day's readings. Some people's problems haunt me. My Humanitarian theme, which I share with her, and maybe even my maleness on top of it, wants to dig in there and fix everything. I do give it to God, but sometimes I have a hard time distinguishing what is God's job and what God wants *me* to do about it. But then another day dawns, and I'm off thinking about another 20 new people I can worry about.

There are other striking differences between the two of us as well. Like I said, I worry. Mom, on the other hand, is a relentless optimist, which, as much as I admire and love her, irks the hell out of me. She loves her life in the huge public arena. I'm a very private person, and while I'm not afraid of large crowds, they're just not my preference. Sometimes at night, much to my dismay, I hear Charlie in my mind, loud and clear, saying, "Someday, Chris, in years to come, you are going to be out there."

"Damn this destiny," I say.

Everyone fantasizes what they might have been, could have been. I did, too, obviously, when I was younger. But I've been much happier since I turned 30 and took a long, hard look. I realized, "This is it, kid." The die was cast a long time ago, and this is my life. It is honorable, and not only have my peers begun to respect my life, but I've finally learned to stop resisting it and start respecting it, too. I'm sure there are times when Mom wishes I were more like her, the natural-born performer, the boundless ball of energy driven to save the world. We all thank God she's exactly who she is, but we all worry about her, too, until I remember that if you took away from her what and who she is, it would kill her. Aristotle was right: "The essence is that which is, and without which it cannot exist."

One of the first times Mom was on *The Montel Williams Show* was before our children were born. My wife, Gina, and I went to the filming. I was in sweat clothes, because I had come from the gym. (I was also going to be a body builder at one time, a lifetime ago in this life.) I was sitting in the front row, and during one of the breaks, Montel put his arm around me and told me to go on stage with my mother. Before I knew it, they had miked me. I was sitting there trying to figure out how I could kill my mother and get away with it. The cameras rolled, and I just began to talk. I did understand later what she means when she refers to "infusion." You just go on automatic pilot. Montel asked me to give a prediction for the next month. I said there would be a gangland fight in the Pavilion Mall in Los Angeles one week later. Within the next four days, there was a gangland fight in the Pavilion. We don't take personal credit for our accuracy, which may be a surprise to everyone. It is just our job. It comes from God, and we are just the conduit. But what did follow was my mother driving me crazy with, "See, I told you that you could do it. People should see what you can do."

Finally I said, out of exasperation, "Shut up!"

Mom, meek as always, said, "Oh, shut up yourself," and that was the end of that episode. Every time I'm on TV with her, on Channel 4 or *Bay City Limits* or wherever, we go through the same scenario. I go through with it but stubbornly fight it, and then I obsess afterwards, being very critical of myself.

My mother is very self-critical, too, and that's why no one can get her to watch tapes of herself. When she's done a show, she's done, and it's on to the next thing. I, on the other hand, go over and over it, thinking that I could have said more, helped more, and so on and so on. Age helps a little, but not a lot. I'll always, I'm afraid, be much more picky than she is.

Another big difference between us is that I don't let go of things, while she is more forgiving—too much, to my liking. I don't forgive, I just nullify the person. I don't hate them, I just wipe them off the slate, and they don't exist for me anymore. Mom often says she really wishes she could be more like this. After what I've seen her do for her family and then practically get decimated, I'm glad to be the way I am.

Mom will proudly say, much to my joy, that I can read for her better than she can for me. But I value her advice, and on those rare occasions when her spirit guide, Francine, gives advice, none of us, including my wonderful wife, ever bucks that. And because it doesn't happen that often, it carries a powerful punch. I know for a fact that a great deal of accurate information about the Other Side has come from Francine, as well as from thousands of hypnotic regressions that prove our theology, and I'm very grateful to her.

"Vive la différence," as the cliché goes, and I suppose that's true. We can only follow our own chart. Someone asked me the other day if I ever resented being born into this family. The truth is, I had to pause before I finally said, "No, not really." I know I chose it. There are other things I resent on a purely human level, but we'll get into that later.

Wherever my mom goes, she is besieged by people. I'm proud of her, but I'm too private for that. Even though she never shows it, compliments and adoration make her terribly uncom-fortable. She says we have to learn to accept and be gracious when people are complimentary. The best I can do is try. It's not that I don't like getting compliments, I just prefer not to put myself in that position in the first place.

The one exception to my shyness about compliments is the letters I get from clients after a reading. Maybe that's because the information they're complimenting me on and thanking me for isn't really coming from me in the first place, so the credit belongs to God, and I just get the wonderful residual pleasure of confirmation that God, through me, made a difference.

Carol, a client from Southern California, wrote:

> I had the most awesome experience. Chris told me I would be moving, and this was shortly after I had purchased a very expensive new home. At first upon hearing this, I was very disappointed. Not too long after the reading, I was walking on a deserted beach, praying for an answer to my dilemma, when I was suddenly hit by a large wave. While cleaning the sand off myself, I noticed an old woman sitting on a nearby bench— both just seemed to come out of nowhere. Moments earlier there was no one there. The woman said to me, "You should listen to Chris." I turned to finish cleaning off the sand, and when I turned back around, the woman was gone. Shortly afterward, I had a lucrative offer for my home and subsequently sold it. Just recently I learned that the house is within six feet of being washed away from its foundation because of erosion. I can't thank Chris enough for saving me from what could have been a very expensive hardship.

Tilli, from British Columbia, said:

> Thank you, Chris, for your amazing predictions and for sharing your gift. Just as you predicted, I did meet someone with the initials J and D with thick dark hair that was longer in the back, age 34, who lives approximately 20 minutes from me, has a son, and who has the same spiritual beliefs I do. You also said that this person had a lot to do with ships and working around water, which is exactly what he does. You were also

completely accurate about my health and the health of my children. I am now getting help from my gynecologist on my female organ imbalance, and, as you suggested, my daughter is getting help with her bowel problem, which you also accurately predicted. Even more amazing, there was an arrest in the arson/murder case I asked about. I want to thank you over and over again for sharing your wonderful gift with people like me. Many, many a night I prayed for help, and through you, my prayers were answered.

And then there was Denise, from Connecticut, whose letter made me laugh:

I am ashamed to admit that I was one of those "nightmare" people that I am sure your mother and you hate dealing with, who argues and shakes her head no during the entire reading. What you were telling me during the reading seemed so far-fetched that I just couldn't possibly imagine that even half of the things you told me would occur. Well, here it is a year and a half later, and everything has turned out exactly as you said it would. Boy, am I ready to eat a lot of crow, starting with my offering a sincere apology to you for ever doubting your words. God bless you, Chris, for your patience with me, your understanding of my skepticism, and most of all, for your wonderful, wonderful insight.

Again, like Mom, I privately squirm when someone compliments me. But when the compliment goes to God *through* me, I'm only too happy to pass it along.

Sibling Relationships

You've probably noticed that I haven't talked about my other siblings much. Mary, my foster sister, was with us until she was

22 (my mother had full guardianship of her from the time she was 6), and Paul is my older brother. We kids have admitted to each other that as far as Mom's treatment of us was concerned, each of us was an only child. We are a very strong, stubborn, actualized family, which doesn't always create harmony, but it does breed success.

I was fond of Mary, and she was my helper as a child, since Mom was working such long hours to support us. Paul has always been internal. We love each other, but we have never been close. I think my mother has given up on the idea of a "one big happy family" scenario, although Paul and I see each other on holidays. One thing I'll say for Paul, though—he has a darling adopted son, Jeffrey.

Mary and Paul, being older, left home before I did, but until then we always had a full house. Mom didn't just raise the three of us, she also raised "houseguests" who came to stay "temporarily" for, in some cases, years at a time. There were eight in all. I have to admit, I was always the one who brought them in, and it was a running family joke that everyone I brought home was only going to stay for two weeks.

I remember bringing home a friend of mine from school. We'll call her Sally. She was pregnant, and she was being abused by both her boyfriend and her family. With Mom's compassionate permission, she took refuge at our house. It didn't take long for Sally's abusive boyfriend to find out about it, and he came over one day while I was out, broke into our house, and tried to beat up my mother. Mom, being the weak, helpless type, picked up a fireplace poker and took her best shot at defending herself. She was almost holding her own, too, but I still thank God I came home soon enough to take over, pull this guy outside, and, let's say, give him some of his own medicine. (To this day, he has never raised his hand to another woman, by the way. I still see him periodically, and he smiles and keeps his distance.)

A Strong Woman

Mom is scary. My brother and I, at 6'5" and 6'6", respective-
ly, have often said that we could be killed defending her, because
if we get into a fight on her behalf, she'll be right in the middle
of it. As I'm sure you've guessed, our family has always had a
good, healthy temper. We'll take a lot, but we don't ever hurt our
loved ones. I have boxed, wrestled, body built, and still get excited by anything physical or competitive. Becoming a husband and
father has calmed some of these dragons, but you still don't want
to get in my face.

There is no doubt that Mom has been a pioneer in her field,
showing the world that you can have the gift and still be from
God. I did resent the time she spent with her readings and classes, but I see it much more clearly now as I worry about not spending enough time with *my* kids. I understand that she really did
suffer from her time away from us, just as she suffers now from
not being around her grandkids enough. She doesn't even have to
tell me that—I see and know that her grandchildren are her life.

Mom has taken Angelia completely under her wing, and my
little girl thrives on it. Gina and I just smile when Mom brings
Angelia on stage with her, and I always tell my wife, "Mom's
grooming Angelia to follow after us"—as if my little girl wouldn't
insist on it anyway and outshine us all! She doesn't stop at being
an invited guest at Mom's speaking engagements, either. When she
decides the situation demands it, she almost takes over. One night
at a Learning Annex lecture, Mom was guiding the huge audience
through a meditation. Imagine the whole family's chagrin when
throughout the meditation, Angelia walked up and down the aisles
scanning the crowd and then returned to the stage to quietly report
to Mom who did and who didn't have their eyes closed.

As for my little boy, Willy, Mom adores him and says he is
an angel from God's heart, and we all agree. Everyone who sees
Willy automatically smiles, because he is all happy grins through

and through. Angelia is moodier than he is, but as I know first-hand, it goes with the gift. No one can make Willy laugh harder than Mom can, and no one can put him to sleep more quickly. He can be the most wide-awake person on Earth, but two seconds of Mom rocking him in her arms, and he's out cold every time.

In case this isn't already obvious, my children are my life, too. When they were born, I cried at the miracle of these precious, healthy souls who decided to come to Gina and me. And Mom nailed to a T what sex, weight, coloring, and temperament each of them would be. Both Mom and Gina "saw" Angelia before she was born, and Mom was there for both births and helped Gina relax through hypnosis. Mom had to hightail it from L.A. in the middle of the night to be there in time for Willy's birth, and I'll never forget Gina looking up at me from her hospital bed at exactly 3:00 A.M. and announcing, "Chris, Mom just drove into the parking lot."

In other words, there's a deep connection between Gina and Mom, and they can be an awesome duo against one man—take it from me! I know from both sides how much they love each other. Mom says, and means it, that she feels Gina is her daughter, and she backs it up with her actions. If Gina and I have an argument, Mom is right there on Gina's side. And as mad as I get, I always remind myself, "Better this than the alternative." Mom is close to Paul's wife, Nancy, as well, but there's a reason for Gina's and Mom's unbreakable bond.

What happened is that I had just come out of a very devastating relationship. We've all had at least one of those, but this was particularly hard for me. I tried to mask the pain by partying and having one new girlfriend after another, while Mom stood patiently by, not saying much but listening to my pain and my tirades about how unfair life was.

After about two years, I finally began to focus again and settle back into myself and my goals. One day I casually mentioned to Mom that I had met this beautiful girl but felt sure she was dating someone else. "This beautiful girl" and I had a friend in common whom Mom knew. I didn't find out until later that Mom got Gina's telephone number from the friend, and—good old Mom— called Gina right up and introduced herself. (As it happened, Gina knew who she was from seeing her on TV.) Gina couldn't imagine why Sylvia Browne was calling her, until Mom explained that this Christopher Dufresne she'd just met was her son. That was news to Gina, and why wouldn't it be, with the different last names? Mom asked Gina if she liked me. Gina replied that she really did, but she thought I was dating someone. Mom set her straight and told her to call me. Gina said she couldn't do that—she felt it was too forward. Mom then ordered her, "Just do it, Gina. He won't do it, he's too shy."

Well, thank God, Gina did. We fell in love right away. I took her to Los Angeles, and it was as if we had always been together. I sometimes have a hard time telling her this, but I would give her and our children the world if I could. They give my life meaning every single day.

Five months after Gina and I met, Mom took us to Acapulco and married us just before midnight on September 9, 1989. Yes, Mom can legally marry people. She is a full-fledged minister, and her church, Novus Spiritus, is registered with the State of California as an accredited, legitimate church.

Ten years and two kids later, we are a very happy family. The best part is that we live three minutes from Mom and Larry (her current husband, and the best of the bunch), and we all travel together, eat together, and sleep over at each other's houses. It is truly an extended family. Larry has been around Mom for 26 years, so we all know him. I reserved judgment until I saw how good he is to my mom, and most of all, how much my kids love "Ol' Poppy."

CHAPTER FIVE

My Start As a Reader

How I started doing readings could be a book in itself. I mentioned before that after school I always worked in Mom's office cleaning up. I also helped with the literature we sent out—stapling, folding, stuffing envelopes, and so on. Say what you will about nepotism, I really did start at the bottom.

So in I came one day, expecting to start folding Mom's writings for our next mailing, when my mother walked up to me and said, "I booked you three appointments today. Your office is ready, and your first client is waiting for you." I didn't have time to strangle her, or even to be all that afraid. Stunned, I glanced quickly around the room—and realized that the staff had been in on this little surprise. I can still see their smiling, expectant faces as I walked my first client into "my office," closed the door, and sat down across from her.

That first session is still a blur for the most part. I can still remember telling that woman, though, that I wouldn't control her life and that I wasn't a physician, but I would tell her all about her life and then she could ask questions. I remember I talked and talked, and I vaguely remember her nodding in agreement. Then it was over, and the next one came in, and then the next one. By the time the last client left for the day, I was wiped out from nerves and a used-up adrenaline rush. I sat there alone for a while, trying to recover, but finally I emerged from my office again, and I'll never forget the staff, all 12 of them, grinning and applauding the minute they saw me. It meant a lot to me that they were so openly pleased about this new development. And, of course, I learned later that my mother had been in her office praying her heart out the whole time, and lighting her old standby white candles.

It wasn't bad that first day, because I'm sure I was in shock. When Mom informed me I already had appointments set up for the rest of the week, I almost threw up. The possibility that I might actually keep on doing this was beyond my comprehension. Here I was, 16 years old, trying to have a life, and I was being thrown headlong into being a reader?! My mother and I had endless conversations—not about how to read, but about the ethics and format of readings. She was pleased at how I handled those first clients, and she reiterated that we are not in control, we only tell clients what we get—nothing more, nothing less. We agreed then as we do now that we are not there to please our clients or tell them fairy tales, but to say whatever comes in *as* it comes in.

People still think to this day that we can make something happen. No matter how specific we are, they want us to lead them. We won't. *Ever.* We also don't want anyone to depend on us for every move they make. That fosters control and cultism.

We are hardly God, but we'd better be more right than wrong. As Mom always says, "A psychic is only as good as their last reading." People have even accused us of researching them before a consultation. I guess that's a testament to our accuracy. Rationally, though, not only wouldn't we or couldn't we do something like that, but imagine the research team it would take to accomplish such a time-consuming effort!

42

Everyone can be read, by the way, but there is a tiny faction of the population that wants a free reading, or just to argue. Their negativity sets up a barrier that no one can penetrate. I will read and cajole them, while Mom just stops the reading and refunds their money. We do reserve the right to refuse service to anyone.

I am very proud that we are licensed by both the state and federal governments and are members of the Better Business Bureau. We've also received recognition in *Who's Who*. We are both licensed hypnotists, as are most of the ministers and spiritual counselors within Mom's church, Novus Spiritus. Montel Williams always warns people when my mother appears on his show, "If you don't want to know, don't ask." The same goes for me. I don't hold back, and I cannot and will not lie.

At any rate, back to the beginnings of my career doing readings. One week led into another, which led into another and another after that, and before I knew it, a year had passed. After the second year, I finally began to catch on that this really was going to be my life. It was more than the fact that I found it satisfying—it was like I had no free will or choice. I questioned myself constantly. What else would I do? What else would be as satisfying? I could certainly make more money doing something else, but would it be me, and would I love it as much as I loved doing readings?

By the third year, at the age of 19, I was pretty well settled in. Between the office staff advertising my services and general word-of-mouth, my clientele began to grow. And then, of course, there was the fact that my mother happened to be Sylvia Browne. I'll never claim that that didn't help a lot. To be honest, it bothered me sometimes, too. I wondered a thousand times, "Would I ever be booked if I weren't her son?" My ego occasionally took quite a beating over that. But Mom was always right there to sit me down and assure me, "I can open the door, Chris, but if you're not good, you won't keep that door open. You don't fool people. They'll find your heart."

When I began to get letters, and word-of-mouth continued to spread, and clients rebooked again for a year later (the soonest I'll allow anyone to rebook), I started feeling more secure. I knew my motives were pure, I cared deeply about each and every client, and the validations were rolling in. "Chris is amazing . . ." "I can't believe how accurate Chris is . . ." "I am so completely impressed with your reading that I am giving my sister the opportunity to experience your beautiful gift . . ." "You are awesomely accurate and a very sincere, loving, and caring individual. I will never forget our session together. It has changed my life for the better in more ways than I can possibly ever tell you . . ."

So why did I have ongoing waves of insecurity? I finally went to Mom—self-confident Mom—and asked her one day, "Mom, are you ever scared and insecure?"

She looked squarely into my eyes and said, "Son, every day of my life." She went on to point out that insecurity can be a good thing, a human trait that makes you try harder and keeps you humble enough to keep your ego out of the way. That made me feel better.

Mom and I also have a few concrete rules:

- Never date a client.
- Never touch a client.
- Be professional enough not to collect "groupies."
- Do not deal with a medical problem without recommending that the client see their doctor.

We have 204 doctors whom we can call on. I know for a fact that my mother has kept many doctors in business thanks to her referrals.

Another rule: Do *pro bono* work. We have to give back. We answer a lot of charity letters, and Mom works on a lot of cases for law enforcement authorities, parents of missing children, special medical and psychiatric referrals, and so on and so on. She is also very devoted to people with ravaging terminal illnesses. She spent some time with Michael Zaslow, the wonderful soap opera actor who contracted ALS, also known as Lou Gehrig's Disease, a month or so before he died, for example. She would never have asked for or accepted payment for that, especially since she felt she profited from it in ways that were far more valuable than money.

A Worthwhile Profession

In the midst of all this, we support a foundation and a church; we pay taxes; we finance mailings, office space, and office equipment; we pay salaries and more taxes and staggering phone bills (when Mom and I do phone readings, we pay for the call); we pay for the tapes we record our readings on and give or mail to clients . . . the list goes on and on. And oh, yes—there's also the little detail of supporting ourselves and our families. Believe me, we privately laugh to ourselves every time someone comments about how "glamorous" our lives must be. But would either of us trade our lives for anyone else's on Earth? Not a chance. Not only because we were destined to do this work, but also because we surrendered to it with love and with total trust in God.

And, always, because of letters like this one from Kim in Colorado:

> Thank you, Chris. Your reading was miraculous to me. I was feeling scared earlier in the day, wondering how and when I would find strength in a higher power than myself. . . . After your call, I now realize *I* have that strength, in God. You are like my guardian angel, and I feel blessed to have had you in my life when I most needed help. Thank you so much for being there and sharing your gift with me.

To be completely honest, there is a part of my work that hurts, and I hear it every day of my life. People can't help it, and I know it is because they love my mom so much. After 17 years of doing readings, I still frequently hear something like, "I really wanted your mother, but I had to wait so long that I took you instead." Or, "Your mother is so great, I just hope you can be as good." I'm not trying to sound like a martyr, but it can be discouraging to be reminded of what a hard act to follow she really is. I've never told her this, because I admire her work as much as I admire her and her life and what she endlessly does for God. I admire how she picked herself up and started all over again and rebuilt her life after her last husband knocked her down so low. Above all, I love her, and she loves me. Love really does overcome competition and that nasty word *jealousy* that we've never felt toward each other—not once. She says that people don't give enough thought to what they say, and when she was just starting out, people didn't think she could be that good because she was so young. Anyway, I keep right on going, and I know it's for all the right reasons.

There's no doubt about it—our lives have never been boring. Boredom is a killer, and my mom and I will never die of that. Things are swirling around us all the time, and the office is always busy and exciting. Also, let's face it, people don't call a psychic when they're happy. A majority of the time all we hear is illness, death, and tragedy. We're sworn to absolute confidentiality about the content of readings, even between each other, although we occasionally discuss challenging cases without ever naming names. If Mom's working on a highly publicized murder case, she'll come to me for a different perspective on it, but the conversation ends right there. So the nature of our work is pretty crisis oriented, but I'm not complaining. When you can help, there is no other high that compares.

I was advised by Mom at a very early age to take my first impression when doing a reading. She was right. It truly is the only correct one. If you think past your first impression, your logical mind enters in and you negate your own ability.

As I was writing this, Gina came to me about a precious ring she had lost. I was too busy and just said, "You'll find it." Then Angelia piped up. "Mama, it's in my room, and when you quit worrying about it, you'll find it." A few hours later, after Gina had put it out of her mind, she went into Angelia's room, and there it was on the carpet.

One day last year as we drove to the airport, I asked Gina if she had her I.D. She said, "Yes." Angelia said, "No, you don't." Gina, not taking anything for granted, searched her purse, and sure enough, it wasn't there. Even *we* have to keep ourselves from saying, "Angelia, how did you know that?"

Oh, the joys of a psychic family.

We travel a lot together, and we spend the majority of our trips laughing together and spending "quality time" with the kids. My sense of humor is dry. My mother can be outrageous. And I never have to wonder where I got my temper. Mom doesn't just get mad, she gets incensed, and when that happens, she doesn't care where she is or who hears her. She is the one person I know, though, who can chew someone out and still make them feel loved and important.

Sometimes I see my mother watching me, and I can almost read her mind—she's wondering if my childhood was stolen like hers was, or if I feel the same pain that she did over not spending enough time with my children. I imagine someday I'll watch my daughter in exactly the same way and wonder the very same things about her.

Such closeness, combined with the family temper, can lead to some blowout fights—we've had some good ones. We are both strong and stubborn. During one particular battle about who-knows-what, she was so furious that she called me an "S.O.B." The instant it came out of her mouth, she realized what she had said, and she was almost expecting it when I came right back with, "You can say that again." We still laugh over that one.

Mom usually tends to keep her temper in check better than I do, though, especially when it comes to skeptics. We were at dinner one night with some TV people. One of the women brought her closed-minded-skeptic husband along, and from the moment we sat down together, he started taunting my mother. She was handling it, but I wasn't. He kept it up, and I finally stood, turned to him, and said, "Either this dinner is over, or we can go outside." He kept his mouth shut for the rest of the evening. Later the group told Mom how they'd loved that, because they didn't like that guy either.

It's worth a separate paragraph to stress that I have no problem at all with *open*-minded skeptics. I just find the close-minded ones unacceptable, and I'll never sit still when someone's dignity is being sacrificed for someone else's enjoyment.

Mom and I are each other's biggest fans, and when either of us is down, we're the first to be there to comfort each other. The other day she had the flu (she never gets sick) and had lost her voice. She called me, frantic, because she had three episodes of *The Montel Williams Show* to do that day, and how could she do them sounding like a frog? I couldn't help but ask, "Who will notice?" She assured me that I wasn't funny, but she was laughing as she said it, because facts are facts. She has always had a hoarse voice, just like her sister and her mother, and my daughter is going to have one just like it. Anyway, frog voice and flu or not, she made it through all three shows with flying colors, as she and I both knew she would. She wouldn't let Montel down for anything.

Now, *there* is a true friendship-love story—not something you see very often in this life. I've seen my mother's loyalty in action all my life, but I've never seen anyone else repay it in kind like Montel has. They have honest, unconditional love and respect for each other that you can see both on and off TV whenever they're together. Other talk show hosts beg her for appearances, but if there's any chance they'd conflict with Montel, they get a flat, resounding, "Thanks, but no thanks." She would never and will never betray the unwritten exclusivity between them, and you'll never see another psychic on Montel's show, except on those rare occasions when Mom drags me on stage against my will.

CHAPTER SIX

Birth of a Church

In 1986, Mom called a family meeting. To put it in context, she was still married to "the thief" at that time. I call him that with good reason—the man almost pulled her down so far she couldn't get up by selling securities for a gold mine without a license, and none of us knew about it because he was always gone. I remember Mom telling him once, "Go and do whatever you want, but don't hurt my people, my foundation, or my church." But I'm getting ahead of myself

So we all sat in the living room, the staff and the family, and Mom announced she wanted to start a church. Everyone groaned. What had possessed her? Didn't she have enough going on? I could tell by the set of her jaw that no one was going to sway her. I liked the idea, but I could see what she was in for—a lot of criticism and opposition. After all, who had ever heard of a psychic church?

I finally said to the group, "It's her choice and her life; let it go." Everyone grumbled, but they began to plunge in. Ministers were recruited and taught the tenets of the belief—a society in which people could see Christ as he truly was and know that God was a good God—a church based in love, *not* revenge. And that's how the Society of Novus Spiritus was born.

Mom's Priorities

Just like there has never been a limit to the number of people Mom can love, there has also never been a limit to her energy when it comes to her priorities—and love of her family is always at the top of her priority list, along with her love of God. Before Angelia started school, Mom saved some money and took us all to England, France, Greece, Rome, Barbados, Hawaii, New York, Kansas City, and many other places—more than I can even remember. She said she wanted Angelia to see the world. I enjoyed it, but I must admit (for the first time) that sometimes I wanted to stay home and enjoy my family and my house, for which I saved up for such a long time. I could have said no, but how can you deny someone who wanted that family travel time so badly? I couldn't. Besides, Gina enjoys traveling, and shopping with Mom is Gina's idea of heaven on earth. There is a little-girl quality about both Mom and Gina, so with Angelia, I essentially have three little girls on my hands. Thank God for Willy. I was beginning to feel outnumbered.

The signal that there may be a trip in the air is when Mom says, "You really are working too hard [she should talk!]. You need a vacation." I try now not to ever act tired around her. For ten years straight, we never went anywhere, and except for Thanksgiving, Christmas, and Easter, we worked seven days a week, 20 clients a day.

People ask sometimes, "How can you always be at your best?" Again, sheer genetics. If Mom and I had to *try* to make this work, it would kill us. It just *is* us. Sure, we can turn this gift down, but it's always there, waiting to be turned on.

My work day starts at 7:00 A.M. I work until 1:30, take a half-hour break, and then work again until 7:00 or 8:00 P.M. It doesn't leave much time for my family, but like my mother, when I'm with them, I'm really *with* them.

It's not easy to be mellow after a whole day of hearing everyone's problems, and it takes me about an hour after my last reading to come back to myself. It's a combination of a tremendous faith in God and a refusal to let the injustices get to you—the illness, the strife, the missing children, and so on. If we didn't believe that this is a classroom of learning for God, we would be crazy. Just when you think you've heard everything, sure enough, the next day you will hear something else that could set you reeling. The emotional side of your brain receives the infused message, but your intellect has to be the controller. If it isn't, you will fall into the same dark hole your client is in. So, after you validate their problem, your intellect takes over, and you gently draw them up to reality and wellness.

To be married to someone who understands your gift is great. Gina is a total believer. Of course, why wouldn't she be? She sees proof all around her every day of her life. But what I mean is that she is always supportive, always cheering me on. We can fight about many things, but my commitment to my destiny is not one of them.

Sightings

I won't do the volume of police work Mom does, nor will I talk to deceased loved ones. Every psychic has that ability, but I'm not ready for all that yet. I do go on haunting investigations with my mother, and to her delight and mine, I pick up the same spirits. I discovered that for the first time on a haunting investigation we did at the Moss Beach Distillery in Northern California for the TV series *Unsolved Mysteries*. For years, the restaurant's employees and customers had been convinced that the place was haunted, and sure enough, Mom and I both contacted the earth-bound spirit of a woman who had died nearby in a car accident decades earlier. She was still there, hoping to locate, comfort, and care for the young son she'd left behind.

Angelia sees spirits with my mother, too. They both have a relationship with a ghost named Johnny Johnson in a San Jose toy store; they shared a spirit sighting in Greece; and they saw the same two ghosts on an old boat in San Diego called the Star of India. One of my favorite Angelia sightings occurred on a trip with Mom to Graceland. Not only was Angelia convinced that Elvis followed her and Mom—not only for part of the tour but also back to their hotel—but she informed my mother with absolute certainty that it's not really Elvis who is buried in the grave with his name on it. Who knows?

Mom's True Success

We are a family that just naturally yells. You never want to stray too far from my mother in a store, or you, God, and every-one else will hear, "Chris, where are you?!" Then you'll hear someone excitedly ask, "Isn't that Sylvia Browne?"

I invariably say, "Mom, please, so many people know you—don't scream like that in stores."

Her inevitable reply: "Then don't wander away. Besides," she rationalizes, "who doesn't know that I yell?" I always think to myself, *If they didn't before, they know now.*

Another person who gets yelled to a lot is Linda, my secre-tary. I've known her since I was seven years old. She was Mom's secretary first, and then Michael took over that post, which he's held for the past 15 years. They are so loyal, it's truly amazing and gratifying to behold. Linda helps me with bookings and bookkeeping. Michael hands Mom her morning coffee and her schedule while I have my Diet Coke, and then we're both off and running. Instead of calling either of them over the intercom, Mom and I just yell, "Linda! Michael!" I'm sure Larry wonders sometimes why we installed such a sophisticated phone system.

Mom worries me sometimes, because she is always lecturing, doing TV shows, writing books, and reading and traveling, but then I see how good she looks and how healthy she is, and I feel better. I'm so proud she's hit her stride after 46 years in the trenches. She has two bestselling book and is about to do her second Pay-Per-View special for cable television. Sometimes I wish I could do as much as she does, but with my kids so small, it's impossible. She could never have done all this, either, when her children were very young. But now, with the exception of missing her grandchildren, she's really free for the first time in her life.

You can't even mention the word *retire* in front of her unless you want a lecture on how the word *retired* has the word *tired* in it, and she won't have it. She says this is her last life here, but I sometimes wonder if she wouldn't come back again if God needed her to go on a mission. This is my last life, too, but I might take an option on a life after this. What that means is that you have graduated, but you can sign up for extra duty to serve God.

I thank God every night for what I have, and more than anything, I pray as Mom does to keep on going. Like her and our ancestors before us, I am blessed with great genetics and unfailing energy.

Being Tested

I have only had two serious bouts with illness. When I was 14, I had such a bad case of mononucleosis that they were going to have to give me a tracheotomy. Mom stayed up with me for ten straight days and nights—she told me later she was afraid I might stop breathing.

But then, she was always there when we were sick. The other time I came close to an *exit point* (one of the five "outs" we give ourselves from this life when we write our charts) was when I was 19 and living on my own. I was scrubbing the floor, the phone rang, and in my hurry to reach the phone, I slid into a sharp point on the tile step, which produced a large gash in my shin. I poured some Jack Daniels on it (I saw that in a movie once) and went on about my business. I was just getting to know Gina then and was taking her to Los Angeles for a few days. We went dancing, and my leg hurt like hell. I wrote it off as a bruise until it started to turn black. I finally decided to go to an emergency room. To make a long story short, I ended up in quarantine at El Camino Hospital in Northern California with a staph infection that was eating through to my bone. I was on a morphine drip because the pain was so intense. I should have known how serious this was when every doctor my mother had ever worked with kept dropping by to see me.

I learned later that she was pulling out all the stops, even though our beloved physician, the late Dr. Marvin Small, had called her and said, "Sylvia, I won't let him lose his leg." She came each day until she had to go to work, while Gina sat with me day and night. It's an understatement to say that I was impressed. I thought, *If Gina can be loyal to me at my worst, what will she be like when I'm okay? What a girl!*

I did get my strength back, obviously, but it was a good lesson that no matter how big or strong you are, you can be temporarily felled by life. It gave me a new respect for my body, too. And I know that times like those are special dots on the charts of our lives intended to make us grateful for being well.

Mom and I both believe that if you don't experience sadness, you can't appreciate joy. Illness makes you appreciate health, and loneliness makes you cherish companionship. Like my mother's guide, Francine, my guide, Charlie, always says, "Everything will be all right."

And then we always say, "That could mean anything." This gift is definitely not for us to use on ourselves.

Mom tolerates this "You ought to know better, being a psychic" attitude better than I do. Don't get me wrong—get her mad and she'll dice you with her mouth, but I'm quicker to speak up against what I consider rudeness. After all, you never hear anyone say to a doctor, "Why are *you* sick, of all people?" I hope by the time my daughter takes over, there will be more respect for the spirituality, if not for the ability.

My Beloved Grandfather

My mother lost Ada C. Coil, her grandmother, mentor, and psychic confidant, when she was 18. I lost my true father figure, my beloved grandfather William L. Shoemaker, when I was 30 years old. I've always been grateful that I had him so long. My mom was never close to her mother. None of us were. She was too mean of a woman. But my mother loved her father, and he loved her so much that you could physically feel it when they were together.

I know it was really for my father that my mother started performing, and he, in turn, was her cheering section. When they were together, they would laugh until they cried. My mother could just lay my grandfather out with her humor, and he could do the same for her.

Mom called him "Daddy," and he called her "Sylvie." She told all of us about ten years before he died that he was very ill, but not to let on, and that included telling his doctors not to tell him anything. I've always been knowledgeable in the area of nutrition, so I plied him with amino acids, chelation, and antioxidants. He was never in any pain, but he began to get thinner and thinner.

It was in April, almost four years ago now, when he finally went into the hospital. Mom and I stood by his bed for six hours. He was totally lucid. He even remarked what a lousy day it was to die, because it was so beautiful outside.

I was filled with more pain than I even knew was possible. A few years earlier, I had lost my friend Curtis, which was hard, but we'll talk about that later. Nothing could compare to this. Mom and I both held his hands, and he told me how proud he was of me and how much he loved me. He looked at my mother and told her how he loved her, and then he said, "The hell of the thing is, Sylvie, who will remember like we do?" I saw pain in my mother's face at that moment that I don't ever want to witness again. I guess, in effect, we both lost our dad.

Except for my mother and me, no one knew that we really weren't right for months afterwards. The day my grandfather died, we walked out into that lovely spring day. There were cars moving and children playing. I heard Mom say, "How can the world not stop for a minute? My father just died."

Hoping there was something we could do or somewhere we could go to ease the pain a little, I asked, "What do you want to do?"

She simply looked up at me and said, "What we are going to do is go to the office and go to work."

That may seem callous to the reader, but the only way you can get through that much sorrow is to throw yourself into serving others. Gina was suffering terribly, too, I know. During her last talk with Grandpa, he said, "Keep me alive for Angelia. She's smart enough to remember me." But we've never had to keep him alive for Angelia—she talks frequently about seeing "Ol', ol' Poppy." Larry is "Poppy"; Grandpa was "Ol' Poppy." Whenever Angelia sees him, we all come running, and sure enough, we can smell the strong, unmistakable scent of his favorite cherry blend pipe tobacco.

It's funny, my mother and I never really discuss it, but about six months ago we were lying on the beach and I said, "Mom, I know we don't talk about it, but there isn't a day that goes by when I don't miss him." I could see her lip start to quiver, and she nodded. I pulled her to her feet and we walked back up the hill, together in our pain and yet alone in our individual suffering.

A Time of Loss

Three months later, my grandmother died. Shortly after that, my mother's two best friends passed away. We were now in a whirlwind of pain. No sooner had we begun to get our breath when Gina's sweet brother Chris had a seizure. He had just become a father, and I had paid his attorney's bills so he could get visitation rights to see his son. (Richard Roggia, another priceless family friend and attorney, helped us with that mess.)

Chris was admitted to Stanford Hospital for an operation. The best specialists were called in. Apparently he had been born with criss-crossed neurological wiring, and I'm convinced that the stress of wanting his baby helped bring it on. Gina, bless her heart, was trying to keep the family hopeful, while Mom and I had strong feelings he was going. In cases like that, we always hope we're wrong.

Mom hadn't been to Chris's hospital room yet and was downstairs watching Angelia when Chris came to her and said he was gone. He wanted everyone to know he was happy, and then he added, "Have them quit rubbing my body. I'm gone."

At that moment, Gina joined Mom and Angelia in the waiting room, and Mom told her about Chris's visit and what he had said. Gina hurried up to his room, and sure enough, everyone was gathered around his bed rubbing his body. Half-hysterical with pain, she screamed, "Quit rubbing him! He doesn't like it! He's gone!"

The funeral was a wonderful ceremony. All of our ministers were there. Mom gave the eulogy, and I tried to be brave for my wife, but damn it, I loved the guy, too.

Shortly after that, Dr. Marvin Small died—our friend of 30

years. "Please, God," I prayed, "make it stop." Of course, we know that all are deceased loved ones are happy, but that doesn't alleviate the void they leave behind, the memories and the love. I have no idea how people survive who don't know there is a wonderful dimension beyond this one. Notice I didn't say "believe." I really mean *know.*

My best friend is Shawn Ambrose, whom I grew up with. There were many other good friends—Ray, Mark, and Rob, especially—who always accepted me and my ability. And then there was Curtis, another of my best friends. He lived with us off and on since he was 14 and was kind of a free spirit. He never seemed happy on this earth, and I'll never forget the way we used to talk for hours and hours. When my mother started her church, he was first in line to become a minister.

One day during a ministry class, Mom warned Curtis not to drive his motorcycle on Highway 17. The next Thursday he died. You guessed it—on Highway 17. I don't feel that he meant to die; he was just meeting his destiny, which proves that no one else can interfere with your chart.

I was away at a body-building training camp in New Jersey, so Mom called my camp counselor and broke the news to him first. All my friends at camp took me into a room and told me what had happened. I felt as if I had been gut-punched. Not Curtis—red-haired, grinning, always-laughing Curtis. He used to yell at my mom, "Who loves you, baby?"

She would call back, "You do, you silly red-headed stepchild."

When a person leaves, there is a hole that no one else fills, but what you can do is stack that hole full of your love and memories of them. Then, at least, that hole doesn't stay the gaping wound it starts out to be.

Picking Ourselves Up

Through all of this pain, we were also coping with the illegal dealings perpetuated by Mom's husband, Dal. We were also going through bankruptcy as a result of his actions, and from back taxes that Dal had not paid. I still feel he got off too easy. It kills me that my mother once again came under fire from those who wondered how she could be psychic and get fooled like that. One thing my brother and I had in common is that we both wanted to whip Dal's ass in the worst way, but the law took care of that for us. Mom, however, picked herself up, worked even harder, and after seven long years, had paid off all the banks, bills, taxes, and so on.

It is horrible to watch someone you love almost go down the tubes after a lifetime of unselfish work, but sometimes you have to just stand back and try to stand strong for them. She didn't just do it for herself, but also for her ministers, her staff, her family, and all the other people who believed in her. She always says, "If you just stay standing, you will survive. After all," she says, "all that matters is what God and you know." And only God, Mom, and I know how she has to make every aspect of her business legal and completely ethical in every respect. She will not stand for any fishy business.

I have only known her to steal once. When we left Gary, Mom's first husband, we just took off—Mom, Mary, Paul, and me. We had no money. I had started school, and I really didn't have any shoes. We went to K-Mart, and Mom told me to try on these little tennis shoes. I put them on, and we walked out. I didn't know until later that we hadn't paid for them. One year after that, she walked back in to K-Mart and gave the clerk $4.95 for the shoes.

Mom's second husband, in my opinion, was an obvious opportunist, but it was always Mom's work that supported all of us. Larry, her present husband, has been around as long as I can remember, and he was always there helping her. She had done a reading for him 26 years ago and told him that one day he would marry an older woman with two kids, but she couldn't see the woman's face. When all this hell broke loose with Dal, Larry helped put our business back together. He and Mom married six years after Gina and I did. My kids just naturally feel he's "Poppy." I am so happy that she has a partner and a manager. Our office was even used by the State of California as an example of how a business should be run. Larry is so picky that not a nickel falls anywhere that he doesn't put his foot on it. The staff sometimes calls him "Scrooge," but better that than the opposite!

The Circle of Life

Throughout our journeys in life, you can see circles within circles—Grandma Coil, my mom, me, Angelia—and then I'm sure it will start all over again. As Mom's grandmother told her, as she has told me, and as I will tell my daughter, there is no greater calling than helping others. It is very important to see someone's life chart, but it is also important to give advice and solace. We are not doctors or psychologists, but we are very much spiritual counselors.

Gina and I raise our children as Mom raised hers, to be truly Christian, which we are. That means that you follow the correct and moral and ethical way to live. What goes around does come around, so it's imperative to set good into motion that will make a circle and come back to you.

I see so much hopelessness, despair, and depression in my readings, and I try to educate people that this world is not where it all is. There is another side—the Other Side. We have seen it in our regressions, counseling for death and dying, and also from my mother's near-death experience and my own astral visits to the Other Side.

Family Love

When I've had a particularly hard day, I look at Angelia's lavender eyes and Willy's ever-smiling face, and I see God. Like every father, I want the best for my family. I have worked hard to give them a home. We still drive an old van, but as much as we travel, who cares?

I consider it one of my greatest accomplishments that I was able to buy my mother a home. She couldn't do it for herself. With the church and all her other expenses, there just hasn't ever been enough money to keep everything going. I wish it could have been a mansion, but *she* doesn't—she loves that house exactly as it is.

Shortly after she moved in, she and Eya (Angelia's name for herself, if you recall) were sitting out in the garage making Christmas crafts. Mom had her hair tied up and an apron on. Eya had on an apron, too, and was wearing goggles. They were painting away and singing (off key) "Santa Claus Is Coming to Town." They didn't know I was watching, and they didn't care that there was more paint on them than on their crafts. That moment still makes my heart smile.

When we were little and something wonderful would happen, Mom would say, "Take a breath and close your eyes and save it." When Mom first saw the house, her eyes were misty and that damned chin quivered. *I* saved it.

Gina's brother left her some money in his will. Rather than pay bills, I bought her a ring with it because I wanted her to have a memory. Her eyes misted over, and her lips quivered, and I closed my eyes and saved that, too.

We were in Cabo San Lucas when Hurricane Faustus hit. We were in the elevator, being herded to the basement of the hotel, when the power went out. I stepped up, and, adrenaline pumping, forced open those elevator doors, at which point Eya announced to everyone, "Daddy is Hercules. He is our hero." Another keeper.

Gina and I sit up at night and just marvel at our kids. We almost say in unison, "How did we do this?" Willy is all boy and weighs 40 pounds at 14 months. He never cries, loves to eat, and smiles all the time. He is into everything. Gina goes crazy trying to keep up with him, and I'm not sure it helps when I rationalize that he's a boy.

I'm afraid I took after my mother in being a clean freak. My grandfather used to say to her, "Why don't you just tie a mop on your tail so you can do two things at once?" My brother is the opposite—Mom used to threaten to bulldoze his room. But she and I always want everything clean. It's compulsive behavior, I'm sure. Thank God Gina loves things to be clean, too. In fact, when Mom takes the kids, Gina and I clean.

My home is much simpler than Mom's. She fills up every corner and every shelf with gifts from clients, mementos from Kenya, and so on and so on. Dusting for her must be a nightmare. More is better for her, but for me, sparse is cleaner. Eya, on the other hand, has every square inch of her room filled with stuffed animals, Barbie Dolls, music boxes, etc. Who says genetics don't reproduce?

Like my mother, I feel that money is only a vehicle that allows us to make others happy and also provides a building for people to work in, a place for people to come and go and get healed, and where ministers can counsel and help people. I personally saw my mother turn down $40,000 a week, just to start, to sponsor a psychic hotline. Without batting an eye (and God knows how badly we needed the money), she said no.

The man who made the offer said, "What do you mean, no?"

Mom replied, "I don't know what I would tell God. Besides, since I couldn't possibly answer every call, the answer is no."

This man called back and told Larry he admired her, but he

had never heard of anyone turning down that kind of money. "Well," Larry explained, "you have *now*." Mom told me later that she had a very long talk with God that night. Temptation can come from any side, but it is never too hard to turn it down when you realize that that type of glitter is not good for the soul.

We are not really a family of meditators, but we do surround ourselves with the white light of the Holy Spirit and ask each day that our channel is clear and untainted by ego. Our church, The Society of Novus Spiritus (Latin for "new spirit"), uses prayer in abundance, but it mostly involves a hands-on approach—working, counseling on the telephone, and visiting the sick and the elderly. A society is stagnant if you don't get out to the people, and our ministers are always online answering spiritual questions both over the telephone and via e-mail.

And we never, ever turn anyone away, regardless of color, creed, or sexual preference. It's ridiculous to believe that God only made some of us but not others. That belief is not only cruel, it's stupid!

CHAPTER SEVEN

Through my mother, I have certainly met my share of celebrities. She is very understated about that. I grew up knowing them, but I never gave it a second thought. They are people, just like everyone else. I can tell you from spending time with "names" and even doing my own share of readings for them that they are just as insecure as the rest of us, and in some cases even more so. They generally want to please, and they hurt, laugh, and cry like all the rest of us. I don't always envy their fishbowl lives, but we have to allow everyone to be who they are. What a dull world it would be if we were all the same.

We never share our mailing list or our client list. My mom has been asked—in fact, begged—to talk about famous clients. You could threaten her life and she still wouldn't do it. There is no amount of money that would make it worth her while or mine to expose a single word that passes between us and our clients. Mom also works with the police, FBI, and families of crime victims. She never discusses the details of that work with anyone—ever—and that goes for me, too.

I have found in dealing with those who are mentally ill, after referring them to any one of our doctors, that they can feel better if you give them consent to be. As for those people who believe that they are cursed, it's sad, but no matter how much we try to educate people, there are still charlatans around who take thousands of dollars to remove a curse that doesn't exist in the first place. You can't even get the victims to release the names of these vultures so you can turn them in, because of their fear of reprisal.

There was an amazing parade of people in and out of our house while I was growing up—psychologists, writers, lawyers, doctors, teachers, artists, celebrities, mechanics, landscapers, house painters, and more. You name it, they found their way to our house, which was only 1,100 square feet. How everyone fit in there I don't know. I used to believe when I was little that somehow the house just magically expanded to accommodate everyone.

This past Christmas, Mom had an open house. Her house is still not huge, yet at one time I counted 95 people. Later, 70 more arrived. My kids loved it, and I did, too, but my nerves were shot after a few hours. New Year's Eve it was the same, so I guess moving into a house means that my mother can finally entertain again. Also, when I was a child, there always seemed to be something cooking on the stove, and there still is. When Mom is home, she cooks and cooks.. I hope someday she has a chance to do more needlepoint, which she is addicted to, and to paint and write as much as she pleases, but I know her well enough to be sure that if there were just one person left who needed her, she would be there. I have heard her say, "I wish I could *divide* me."

I was walking through the office one day, and I overheard one of our staff saying to a client, "Yes, dear, I know, but if we load them up any more, we won't have time to do *anyone.*" That gave me food for thought: You *do* have to have time for family, and maybe this is what is behind my mom's madness to always want to take us all somewhere.

Both Mom and I are into nutrition and natural hormone replacement. I'm convinced that it works—I can see it on her. She looks younger than her almost 63 years. The only problem is that I know that she feels she has lasted longer than her peers. She was very much enamored with a gay teacher she once had, Bob Williams, who encouraged her to go public with her gift before he died. Our late attorney, Marvin Small, was such a great help to my mom when she was raising us alone. Her father, mother, and friends have all passed on, and on it goes. In lighter moments, she laughs and says that these are the same people who said she couldn't keep running as fast as she does and last. But to put it mildly, she has. We both have stubborn, strong wills. We don't believe in letting illness get us. We know it's a combination of taking care of ourselves with the help of marvelous doctors and advancements, and the truth of mind over matter. So far it's working.

With our jobs, Mom and I need external activities to focus on to keep our minds quiet because it can get too noisy inside sometimes with so much input. So, for example, we both enjoy changing our looks periodically. Sometimes I let my hair grow, then I shave it all off (a la Montel Williams), and Mom goes blonde. We also love changing our rooms around. In fact, my mother calls my house the Winchester Mystery House because I keep adding on.

Mom is on the road a lot, so I bitched at her until she got two superb bodyguards—not because of death threats, but because she literally gets mobbed when she's out. Once in Seattle she got separated from Michael and Larry, and hundreds of people rushed her. The ministers and staff, horrified, scrambled to protect her, and to this day when you mention it, they all shudder at that memory of how she almost got trampled on. She usually doesn't panic, but that incident shook her up enough that she finally gave in. She has never wanted people to feel she was unapproachable, but she couldn't come up with an answer when I asked, "What are you going to do if 4,500 people decide to rush you?" Her bodyguards are well trained and very efficient, and more important, they love Mom.

One of them, Jim, always calls me after every lecture and says, "I got her to the hotel safely." We have never really received hate mail, though. I know that people appreciate her spirituality and her Christ Consciousness, and Mom never steps on anyone else's beliefs. She has studied theology all her life and is an expert in Bible studies. She also taught in the Catholic school system for 18 years, and it's just a good idea not to ever attack either one of us when it comes to our relationship with God.

My theology is rooted innately in my soul. You do good, because the alternative is a dead-end street. I try to make sure every day that I help others through this noble profession, and it makes me feel good. Like our Lord said, "We should all be fishers of men."

I never tread on my mom's domain, nor does she tread on mine. This is called respect. Many have asked me if it isn't difficult working with my mother, or, more specifically, another psychic. The answer is, "Never." I'm my own agent and my own person. Most of us feel self-employed under this umbrella of faith we all share. If you have the same focus on spirituality and you love and respect each other, competitive discomfort isn't even an issue.

If there is a problem, Mom is usually the bottom line that fixes it. The staff has been criticized for protecting us too much, but has anyone thought what it would be like if there weren't any stopgap? For example, once the staff kept getting annoying calls from a guy in Chicago whose point seemed to be, "You people are frauds. You just *think* you're psychic." Michael was on the phone with him one day, trying as best he could to be polite (Mom's policy is, "Courtesy comes first, but you don't ever have to take disrespect from anyone"). Mom happened by during the call and asked, "Michael, who is that?"

He replied, "It's that dick from Chicago."

Mom took the phone receiver from Michael and said, "Listen, Dick, don't call here anymore." She then noticed the staff waving their arms like mad and laughing. When she got off the phone, they informed her that the man's name was Bill. Michael's calling him a "dick" was an opinion, not his name. But thanks to Mom, the man never called again.

I'm definitely more self-conscious than my mother is. She doesn't care what she says or where, and she'll make faces, roll her eyes, and give looks that can kill. She *is* a lady, but her candor makes me cringe sometimes. I tend to be socially aware about propriety, until and unless I get mad, when I'm told that my eyes turn from blue to black. When I was younger, I couldn't shake it off, but I have learned to control it better.

Mom never left us kids with strangers. When we lived in a duplex next door to her family, my Aunt Sharon watched us. Later Mary, who was older, watched us. It was always family or extended family who took care of us, and now Gina and I feel the same. If it's not Mom and Larry watching our children, we'll drop off Eya and Willy at the office for a few hours, which the staff loves—lunch with Daddy and Grandma; typing with Linda; coloring with Michael; playing with Tina, Bea, Mary, Christina, Pam, Sharon, and even my grandpa before he died—not to mention the ministers who spoil them, hold them, bring them presents, and shower them with love. Mom's two Yorkshire Terriers, Toto and Teddy, are at the office as well, as were Angel and Silvie, her two Burmese cats, until they died. No wonder people come into the office and feel a sense of home, peace, and love. Sometimes people come in just to hang out because the energy is so comforting there.

I have my house situated so I can do telephone consultations from my home office a few days a week. It's great, because the kids and Gina like to know that I'm in the house, and for that matter, so do I. Mom does readings from her house as well, but she goes to the office more often than I do because of minister meetings and trance sessions, when her guide, Francine, comes in and talks about theology and the direction of society.

Contrary to what you might think, when we go out with friends socially, we don't just sit there and be psychics all night or try to second-guess each other. Someone asked Larry once if he asks my mother questions all the time. He answered, "Yes, I ask her, 'What's for dinner?' or 'Where are my socks?'"

The other day my mom called, and Eya answered the phone. Mom said, "Is Gina there?"

Eya said, "No."

Mom paused and said, "Oh, I know, she went to the dentist."

Eya asked, "How do you know?"

Mom replied, "Eya, I'm psychic."

Eya came back with, "I didn't know you were that good."

When my kids get sick or hurt, I'm not ashamed to admit that I am a mess. Even when Eya got her ears pierced at three months of age, I seemed to feel it. I'm sure the psychic mind is more empathetic, but with our clients we have to try to stay sympathetic rather than empathetic. If we get too close, it pulls us in, and we feel like we're drowning. In fact, Mom and I have such a bond, as she did with her father, that if we have anxieties, we're not always sure whose angst it is, mine or hers. Usually, if something upsets her at 2:00, by 3:00 I'm uneasy, and vice versa.

It is hard to please people and help them and still stay true to your infused knowledge. If you tell clients something they don't want to hear, they will sometimes argue with you. I've wondered more than once why they bother. If they already know the answers, then why do they call me? This has happened so often, and then I'll get a letter apologizing for how wrong they were. A perfect example came from Diane in Washington: *"I am so sorry I argued with you, Chris. You turned out to be exactly on the money on nearly everything I asked. I just couldn't see it at the time."* It would be so much easier if people listened, asked questions, and then waited to see how the future played out.

By and large, though, people really are becoming more educated. They realize that we are just the reporters, and they (and God) are the editors. How many of us would have believed ten years ago, or even two, that we would be where we are at this point in our lives? Even Mom said she hadn't really believed her psychic grandmother when she told Mom that she would get married, move to the West Coast, and have two boys—after all, at that time my mother had her heart set on becoming a nun. But lo and behold, Mom got married, moved to the West Coast, and had my brother and me.

Time seems to be going so fast, and I am not the only one who feels this way. My clients—young, middle-aged, and old—say the same thing. Even my kids feel it. Do I believe in the end of things? Of course I do, but I know it's not going to happen anytime soon—at least not in the next 100 years.

Like Mom, I believe that we are in an age of spiritual awareness. People are searching for truth *en masse*, when the truth really lies within themselves. It's like a rabbi once said. "A man looks up to God and asks, 'Why did you send so much suffering? Why don't you send someone to help us?'"

And God answered, "I did send help. I sent *you*."

Gina and I were thinking about having more children, but we have decided against it. There isn't enough time or money. Besides, as Mom pointed out, "Quit while you're ahead," and when it comes to how blessed we are with Eya and Willy, we are *definitely* ahead. I wanted a house full of children, but that will happen—I am very aware that I will have six grandchildren. You see, there are a few things we know about ourselves. But if you had someone telling you every day what lies ahead, what would be the joy in living? We write our blueprints before we come here, but we also put our own modified designs and colors into them. And that is why we won't read for the same people over and over again. Mom and I both have clients we have had for years, but they might get a reading every five years, or two at the most.

Do we miss? Of course we do. Only God is perfect. When Mom was on *A.M. LA,* she predicted the Los Angeles earthquake but missed it by four days. You guessed it—we got caught in it. Mom said it was a sign to keep her humble. When it hit, I was sleeping in the living room, Gina was in the bedroom with baby Eya, and Mom was with Larry in their bedroom. It was 4:31 A.M., and it jolted us so hard I hit the floor running, on sheer primordial instinct, yelling out to Gina in the jet-black darkness. After a few almost operatic high notes of terror that she'll never be able to duplicate again, she yelled back that she and Eya were okay. So I started for Mom's room and ran right into her running down the hall. It took awhile before Larry and I would let her come into the living room to see the destruction of so many of her prized Kenya collectibles.

After what seemed like hours of blackness and nonstop sirens, the sun came up, and soon after that my brother called from Northern California to see if we were all right. When he asked to talk to Mom, I said, "She's not here."

Paul said, "What do you mean, she's not there?!"

I told him the truth: "She went to have her nails done."

Mom said that if this was it, this was it, but at least she would go down looking nice. You figure it out! People still don't believe me when I tell that story, but thank God, I had witnesses.

I often marvel at the human machine that puts you into action without thought. It is pure caveman instinct. One part of your brain says, "Family in danger, save them," and your body just leaps to react.

So, hurricanes, earthquakes, the L.A. riots—all part of life's little vignettes to make us appreciate what we have. I had a friend who moved from L.A. to Kansas because he was afraid of earth-quakes, and a tornado hit his house. So much for destiny.

Sylvia at age 16.

Sylvia, prior to a live stage performance as Becky Thatcher in Tom Sawyer *in 1957 (at age 21).*

Sylvia with her two sons, Chris (left) and Paul Dufresne, in 1969.

Chris's daughter, Angelia (Eya), pumpkin shopping in 1994.

Angelia posing in vintage clothing in 1999.

Ada, Sylvia's beloved grandmother, bears a striking resemblance to Angelia. The family believes that Angelia is Ada's reincarnation.

Sylvia and Angelia during a photo shoot for Cosmopolitan *magazine in 1995.*

Chris's wife, Gina, with their daughter, Angelia, Halloween 1995.

Chris and Gina in October 1996.

Chris and his mom at Sylvia's 60th birthday party, October 1996.

Angelia, all dressed up for the 60th birthday party.

Angelia, Chris, and baby William in December 1997.

Sylvia and Angelia, Christmas 1997.

Baby boy William at 5 months (already 25 pounds!), named in honor of Sylvia's father.

Angelia, Chris, and Gina in Mexico in 1996.

Secretary Linda Rossi, Sylvia, Montel Williams, baby William, Gina, and Chris in the Green Room prior to one of Sylvia's appearances on The Montel Williams Show.

Chris, Gina, William, and Angelia in Monterey, March 1998.

William and Angelia on an outing, June 1998.

Chris answering questions from the audience following one of Sylvia's lectures in Sacramento, July 1998.

Sylvia, Chris, Gina, and Angelia in Alaska, August 1998.

William and Chris in Alaska.

The audience at one of Sylvia's lectures giving her a standing ovation, March 1999.

William with his "Poppy," Sylvia's husband, Larry Beck, February 1999.

*The little cowboy at home,
April 1999.*

*Too cute for words—
William in the bathtub,
1999.*

A loving granddaughter and grandmother—what a beautiful sight!

CHAPTER EIGHT

Past Lives

The subject of past lives is very important to Mom and me because past lives really do contribute significantly to who and what we are today. Everything from chronic illnesses to latent artistic abilities to phobias can be traced through past-life therapy to cell memory in the soul, and cell memory has a very real impact on each and every one of us. Once the cell memories we're holding have been identified, the soul can view them, understand them, and release them.

We all change themes through different lifetimes, but I know I've kept a warrior theme through many lives, when I was a gladiator, a centurion, and even a king. Either I didn't handle that theme well and need to keep working on it to perfect for God, or I just like it.

I have had 47 lives. Mom has had 54. One person having more past lives than another has nothing to do with that person being "better." The number of lives we live is only determined by how much we want to experience in the service of God.

I was asked recently if my mom and I were psychic in past lives as well, and in our cases, the answer is yes. I was psychic in four of my lives, and Mom has been psychic in more than half of hers. So, you see, we do pick our lives in ways that help us be genetically predisposed to whatever our mission is here.

I can't remember a time when I doubted, even for a minute, that I had lived before—probably because I've always had specific memories of some of my past lives. As I mentioned earlier, I knew as a child that I had previously been a cowboy, but I also knew I'd once been a man whose family was lost to me in a fire. That left me with an almost unreal fear in this life of my house burning down, until Mom did hypnotic regression on me and helped me release that fear by showing me specifically where it came from.

Mom will be the first to admit that she was more reluctant during *her* childhood to give much credence to the concept of past lives. She attributes that reluctance to her strict religious upbringing, but I believe it has more to do with her tendency to insist on researching everything extensively and seeing proof with her own eyes before she chooses what to believe and what to disbelieve. The concept of past lives has been proven to her beyond any doubt now—after a lifetime of research. To say that my mother believes in reincarnation is an understatement.

We come back into each new lifetime with a different purpose or theme, to experience many varied situations that will help us serve God. We might go through just one lifetime on Earth, or twelve, or sixty—the number of incarnations we choose to have has nothing to do with our "status" as an entity. It's our free will choice on the Other Side to come here or not to come here on our path toward gaining more wisdom. As Mom puts it, God is knowledge, and we are the experiencing side of God's knowledge.

It's a source of irritation to both Mom and me to hear people say that we have to have many lives because we've been bad, or we suffer in one lifetime because we've caused suffering in another lifetime. We're all here to learn through negativity, and to advance in experience on God's behalf—it's that simple. The more our souls know, the more they expand, and the more we're then *able* to know.

And finally, again based on our own free will, a time will come when we choose to go Home to the Other Side and stay there for the rest of eternity, still living and learning for God but without the negative ego-driven nonsense we subject ourselves to here on Earth. I tell myself often that I'm done after this life, but I can also picture myself choosing another life, just to see the end of things. When I say that to Mom, she rolls her eyes and says, "Don't ask *me* to come back here again!"

We'll see.

A Shared History

Most of us in our family and extended family, including the staff and ministers, have had a past-life history together and will even tell the same stories, independent of each other, under hypnotic regression. Several of us were early Gnostics, the religion Jesus practiced. Mom and Kirk, one of our employees, were brother and sister in Qumran, where the Dead Sea Scrolls were written. Gina and Mom were together, with me, during the time of Eleanor of Aquitane. We all seem to have come back again— not to recruit, but to show the world Christ's words of love and nonjudgment.

When fear and control are the ruling emotions in a group, you get cultism such as Waco and Jim Jones' People's Temple. We will have more of that before this year is over, a few power-mad people taking advantage of the millennium panic and collecting well-meaning followers by convincing them that their "leader" is, in reality, God. There is only one God, of course, and He doesn't collect people; He just unconditionally loves.

I was buried alive once in a past life, unable to save my family, and I came into this life with a leftover cell memory of that death. Learning that has made it easier to put the horror of it in its proper timeline. Mom and I see lots of clients with past-life phobias who have found their way into this life—a woman afraid of water who drowned in a past life, a controlling husband who was a father to his wife in a past life, and so on. When we give those clients this truthful information, they can release it. The soul cannot be fooled by a fairy story.

When we took Eya to England, she was convinced that she *should* live there and *had* lived there, and she stated we should "get that old lady out of there" (the queen). She *did* seem to understand when we told her that she was reacting to a past life. She also responds to Atlanta and seems to know and love it. My wife, Gina, had a life in New York in the early 1900s, and she still gets a rush every time we go there.

As mentioned previously, Mom is convinced that Eya is the reincarnation of Grandma Ada. I wasn't skeptical when she first talked about it—I just thought maybe her emotions were understandably getting involved. But when Eya began to relate episodes that only Grandma Ada and Mom could know, I took serious notice. The examples are too numerous to list here, but a perfect one happened when Mom took us back to her hometown of Kansas City, Missouri, where she had spent 27 years with Ada. We were driving down a street known only to my mother when Eya (as a very young child) suddenly sat up and screamed, "Bagdah!" (her name for Mom), followed by, "Daddy, stop!" I did. She turned back to Mom and pointed to an old brownstone building. "Remember, Bagdah?" My mother smiled but didn't coach her, as Angelia went on to recall that she used to carry my mother across the street from that brownstone to a grocery store.

Mom looked calm, but I could feel her growing excitement. "Yes, Eya," she said very quietly, not wanting to scare her off the subject, "you *did* carry me across the street to a Kroger grocery store." There was nothing but a vacant lot where the grocery store once stood.

Eya went on to say, "Remember when I made you night-gowns?"

"Yes," Mom replied, "and they scratched my neck." That was it. That one episode was over as soon as it began, but there were many, many more, and I'm now completely convinced.

Astral Projection and Other Gifts

Astral projection should never be used as an escape from anything—my using it to avoid math class taught me that child-hood lesson very well. But for research into the Other Side, for reunions with deceased loved ones, for a safe break from the weight and density of our bodies, and for absolute assurance that the soul is its own separate, living, and eternal entity, astral pro-jection can be a truly joyful experience.

My little Eya not only has kinetic powers, but she's able to astrally project as well. If she doesn't like something, or if it frightens her, she just slumps over, gives a little jerk, and lies very still until the unpleasantness has passed—for example, the Pirates of the Caribbean ride at Disneyland scared her. She jerked asleep the instant she felt afraid, and as soon as the ride was over, she was awake and back to her old self. Gina, concerned, looked at me and said, "Chris, what was that about?"

I said, "It's astral projection. I did it all the time when I was little, especially in math class."

Eya's signal when something is unpleasant is, "I'm tired," which means she wants out. My mother and I often worry about other children with this same ability whose families don't under-stand what's happening, and with all the best intentions, end up stifling the child's gift.

The way to handle this situation is to listen to children's sto-ries, even if they sound like fantasies. Never use the word *imagi-nation*. Never discourage them from telling you about the things they see, even if you don't see them yourself. Animals and children see things, hear things, and know things that the average adult has been trained by our Earthly society not to believe in. Eya and Mom, by the way, can talk endlessly about Kenya and Egypt, where Eya has never been in this life. Angelia wants to see the "bonies" (skeletons), and she knows more about the tribes than many African Americans. She can tell the difference between a Masai, a Samburo, and a Kikuyu tribe at a mere glance.

When Eya did a short stint on an *Evening Magazine* filming with Mom at the Winchester Mystery House, my heart just swelled. She came in on cue and focused on the same spirit Mom was talking to, and then they would turn to each other and compare notes. Gina cried, and I had an ostrich egg-sized lump in my throat. Silently, feeling the warm glow, I said, "Are you watching, Grandpa?" And of course he was.

Needless to say, I didn't know my mother at the age Angelia was that night, but between the two of them, I knew I was watching the unquestionable magic of genetics—their identical candid throaty speech, hands planted firmly on hips, the tempestuousness, and the sense of humor. It really is strange how the psychic gift will jump around in families—Mom's grandmother, but not her mother or sister; me, but not my brother; Eya, but so far not Willy. Only in Ada's family were there two in one generation—Ada and her brother Henry—but they were two of a total of five children. Mom and I each have had two children. Maybe if we had more, it would show up again. Only God knows. I do feel that since it was Grandma Ada who brought our genetic gift to the U.S. (her ancestors were from Germany) and fostered Mom's abilities (Mom, in turn, fostered mine; and I, in turn, am fostering Angelia's), it seems logical that Ada would come in through Angelia to complete the circle.

Will Angelia's children have this gift? Possibly. Mom and I both feel that there are only 100 years or so left to this planet (because we've destroyed our rain forests and other natural resources). No doomsday, no Armageddon—it will just end quietly as we all pass to the Other Side. So after Angelia, there would be enough time for at least one offspring and the possibility of that offspring at least getting a spiritual footing by having another psychic child. That would mean three generations of psychics co-existing with each other, as with Mom, me, and Angelia.

There are so many souls coming in with a *mission* now, asking more than they ever have, "What can we do to make the world better?" I feel that people are sensing that this is the Age of the Messiah—the spiritual age when humankind turns to help each other and seeks vigilantly for the God-center of their own eternal souls.

CHAPTER NINE

Unconditional Love

To those of you who are reading this book hoping for a juicy, never-before-told exposé on my mother—forget it. She doesn't need me or anyone else to do an exposé on her. She does it herself, all the time, and never holds anything back. Her failures, her blind trusts, her ignorance or stupidity on some personal matters in her life are all there to read, or you can just ask her about it and she'll tell you. To have Sylvia Browne as a mother is a hoot—at the same time embarrassing, wondrous, and a blessing. She is my friend and confidant, as I am hers. I love her as I know she loves me—as she puts it, "beyond love's own power of loving," and that is a beautiful feeling.

Her grandmother said many wonderful things to her that she has passed along. One in particular that I love is, "Within your weakness, there lies your strength sleeping." Another is, "My heart would hear you and beat if it lay for a century dead."

Our lives are truly like building blocks, one upon another. We each have to hold fast, not give up, and for God's sake, not let our blocks crack. As I've stated, it seems as if there are circles within circles in life. A mother and father protect their children (I know this more fully now that I'm a parent myself), and when the child grows up with love and, perhaps, divine luck, the child protects the parent. I saw my mother do this when she supported her parents in their later years, although I felt she was a parent to them even when she was a child. As I've grown older, I have been surprised that as strong as my mother is, she has often exhibited the need for my protection.

Mom was traveling, as usual, when, during this particular flight, a young, tall, large-boned male purposely tried to trip her. She knew it was deliberate, but she kept quiet. As she was leaving the plane, he swung his duffel bag at her and hit her—he knew who she was, and out of ignorance, had decided she was an agent of the devil. She looked him in the eye and said, "When I get off this plane, my son is going to get you."

Truthfully, sometimes I met her flights and sometimes I didn't, because of my schedule. But that night I was having dinner with Gina when I had an overwhelming urge to get to the airport, not knowing until later that during the whole trip from Seattle after Mom's first encounter, she had kept sending the message, "Chris, please meet this plane." I was sitting with Gina in the waiting area when Mom bolted through the door, her brown eyes wide as saucers, and said breathlessly, "Chris, see that guy over there? He tripped and hit me."

All I heard was, ". . . hit me." The guy was heading to a pay phone. I walked over to him, and just as he was beginning to dial, I put my finger on the receiver button of the phone.

The guy looked up, startled, and said, "Who are you?"

I calmly replied, "I'm someone who came to shut your world off."

He turned around and saw Mom and immediately turned

white as a sheet. She said, "I told you my son would get you." At that moment, she seemed just like a little girl, saying, "My daddy can beat up your daddy." By then he was stuttering and shaking.

I observed, "You can be very brave while you're pushing a woman around."

He said, "I'm so sorry, sir," and the front of his pants began to get wet. We both felt sorry for him at the same time.

I said, "Apologize to her." He did, profusely.

As she walked away, I heard her tell him, "Let that be a lesson to you. When you're cruel to someone, you never know who may be waiting for you at the end of the line."

I was very proud that I was there, able to protect and defend her, but very surprised at the same time, because she had never asked that of me before. I feel that this incident marked a change in our relationship and drew us even closer. She is not at all helpless, and she has a temper, but it meant a lot to me that she trusted me enough to not only right a wrong, but to do so without losing my head.

When I decided to write this book about my life with Sylvia Browne, I was at a loss at first about what to say. How can you be objective about your own mother? But then I realized that we are all many things to many people, and I, as her son, cannot and will not even try to keep the interwoven threads of our lives separate.

Mom's eternal optimism comes with an underlying wisdom and sadness. I understand that, because it goes with the territory. She is truly shy, which might surprise you, and she's insecure about many things, with the exceptions of her knowledge of God and her ability. She has a razor-sharp wit, and her sense of humor is superb, of course. And she can be so stubborn you may want to scream, but reason can sway her.

Mom prefers being around men more than women, although she has many women friends. She may not see this, but I do—she was close to her father and her grandfather, and she raised male children, so it's natural for her to be predisposed to males.

I am absolutely certain, as is anyone who sees her, knows her, admires her, loves her, or even dislikes her, that there is no one quite like her. She teaches the lessons she lives—to be our own person, to follow our destiny, and to treat every person with respect, regardless of color, station, or creed, unless and until they prove themselves unworthy of that respect.

I see Mom rounding a corner in her life now. I wish it could have happened sooner, because she has worked tirelessly for God for so long. But better late than never—her time to shine truly has come.

And as she turns that corner, it continues to be my great joy that she keeps Angelia right by her side to share it with her, and they're growing closer day by day. Mom has plans to take Eya on three more Learning Annex tours this year, which my daughter loves. As audiences have grown bigger and bigger, we've adopted a type of lottery system—it became bedlam when everyone wanted a question answered—so now we draw tickets, which is more impartial and gives each person a fair chance. When Eya tours with Mom, she goes on stage with her and pulls the numbers out of the box, and she'll even sit on Mom's lap while she answers audience members' questions. I know that when Willy gets older, she'll take him, too. Knowing Willy, he'll be just as happy on the road with her as he is at home with us—smiling and eating and being a big baby boy.

When Mom took Eya on her most recent lecture tour, she sat her down before they left and said, "Now, Eya, I want you to be nice while we're on this trip, because I certainly don't want to spend three days yelling at you." Eya looked right back at her and said, "Well, then, don't." The women in our family have never been at a loss for comebacks.

Gina loves family, too. She remarks often about how wonderful it is for our kids to grow up with so much exposure to life's rich experiences. She's a wonderful, patient mother who puts her family at the center of her universe. Mom said one day, "I have never seen a woman who enjoys every moment of being a mother as much as Gina does." That, I think, is the highest of compliments in this day and age.

No family is perfect, and ours is certainly no exception. Me without a dad to look up to, Mom with a mother who by all accounts was a nightmare. . . . but looking at us, I've decided that one loving parent really can make things good, and I'm determined to prove, with Gina, that two loving parents can make things *great*.

I don't believe you can blame either your failures or your successes on whether or not you've been abandoned or abused or neglected as a child. Life is about rising above these things and then making it better when your turn comes. Mom said to Gina and me a long time ago, "You'll make mistakes just like I did, and you'll learn and do better and even make *different* mistakes."

So, as Mom still says to this day, "Get over yourself." I used to indulge in a fantasy of taking my family away to a more rural area where life would be simpler. But then what would we do?! No, one way or another, you can't perfect your soul without staying in touch with humanity. (Spoken like a true Humanitarian, huh?)

Throughout this writing process, I keep asking myself why I really said yes when Reid Tracy, the vice president of Hay House, approached me about writing a book about Mom. As I mentioned earlier, what could I say that she hasn't and won't? If you don't believe me, just ask her any question about anything. But the real reason I finally agreed is that I *do* have a unique perspective on her, a side of her that is personal to me and no one else. It's exactly what my grandfather said to her right before he died: "Who remembers what *we* remember?"

Adding to our closeness in this life is the fact that we had an especially profound previous life together in France. In that life, I was a king, and very temperamental and combustible. So when Mom accuses me of acting like her father and a king at times, I just say it's a carryover in my cells.

This cell memory theory and the left-brain/right-brain concept were her babies long before anyone else ever wrote or thought about them, by the way. We've had great success healing past-life phobias during regressive therapy by applying cell memory principles.

Back to present-life memories of Mom, though, so many of which still make me laugh. For example, when Paul and I were very young, we sometimes seemed to need the most attention from her when she was in the bathtub. One day he and I got into a major wrestling and screaming match all over the house. To be fair, she yelled plenty of warnings at us to knock it off, but we kept it up. The next thing we knew, she had bolted out of the tub, grabbed a wooden spoon, and starting chasing us. I ran from her for a second until, I couldn't help it, I started to laugh. Then Paul joined in, and finally so did Mom, as it hit us that she was racing around after us with that spoon—buck naked.

We also loved barging right into the bathroom while Mom was in the tub just to tell her about our day, what had happened, what hadn't happened, the funny things—basically, the trials and tribulations of being little kids. She was a great audience at those times, and a captive one, too. One day I traipsed right in on her with four of my kindergarten classmates who wanted to see if my bragging was true—that she really could get rid of warts. I still remember how confused I was that she frantically grabbed for a towel to cover herself. She was in the tub, and my friends and I wanted to chat about warts. What was the big deal all of a sudden?

Mom didn't get physical with us very often, and when she did, I'm sure we deserved it. I don't even know what I'd done one day that caused her to hit me on the arm, but I do know that I promptly announced I was going to call the child abuse center.

She marched right into the kitchen and wrote down the number for me. I'm sure I was thinking, *Now what?* But, stubborn as hell as I was, I just set my jaw and said, "I'll call them later."

And then there was the chaos that would happen every time Paul and I needed haircuts. We didn't have the money to pay a barber, so Mom assumed that responsibility herself. A psychic she is, a hair stylist she is definitely not. All she had to do was reach for those scissors and a comb, and Paul and I would head for the door at a dead run. One day she managed to grab Paul first, while I made a successful escape. I can still hear her calling after me from the open doorway, "You have to come home some-time!" At least when we got older and got jobs, we were able to pay someone to cut our hair. What an incentive to drive someone into the work force—either be gainfully employed or let Mom turn herself loose on your head.

We really could and did talk to Mom about anything, whether she was in the tub or not—school, girls, fights, trucks, shock absorbers, you name it. I look back now and wonder if she really enjoyed all that as much as she seemed to. Sometimes ignorance really is bliss.

But when we were very young, we couldn't return the favor and be the listeners for her that she was for us, especially during her heartaches. I remember one day when she just bundled us all up and took us to Monterey for two days. Not until much later did I find out she was in the process of breaking up with Dad. All Paul and I knew or cared about is that we were on another great adventure with Mom.

I think—I hope—that it's a compliment to Mom that I do sometimes wish I were a kid again. I loved life and people more than I loved school, but most of all, I loved sports. I've always challenged myself and been competitive, which I also see in my daughter, and I'm told it's a long-standing family trait. My great-great grandmother wasn't just a psychic, for example, she was also one of the first female doctors in Germany. And my grandfather, who started out as a mailman, became the vice president of the second largest trucking line in the U.S. He even had a run-in with Jimmy Hoffa. My grandfather was opposed to something the teamsters were in favor of. Hoffa said to my grandfather, "You could find yourself floating down the Hudson River, Shoemaker." To which my grandfather allegedly replied, "And you'll be holding my hand." So much for the good ol' days.

If you're a parent, you'll know what I mean when I say there are times when things are so hectic that I wonder how my mom survived having children, and how and if I will. That's when I'm most aware that when there's a problem, Gina and I will face it together. Somehow, to my growing amazement, Mom faced it alone. For the majority of my life, it was just Mom and us. I hope she knows how much I admire her for that.

And maybe it's a grandmother thing, but my mother has infinite patience with my kids. Eya loves Mom's stories about Africa and about our family history. It reminds me a lot of the ancient tradition of the family matriarch grooming the youngest female to remember the heritage and richness of their ancestry and pass it down.

It makes me both laugh and cringe at Eya's outspokenness when people approach Mom, and Angelia chimes in, "I've been on television, too!" Indeed she has, on *Northwest Afternoon ABC* and *The Montel Williams Show.*

People think it looks so easy to be in that chair, but take it from me, it's very hard. Mom doesn't show it, but I know she gets nervous, too. Oddly, sometimes the more insecure you are, the more you push to perform, so the more confident you look. I'm not insecure about my ability, just about being in the spotlight. But we're a strong group, my family—quick to get angry and quick to laugh—and we're also stubborn, sensitive, and, above all, loyal. We definitely have faults, but faults in some people can be virtues in others. And there have been times when our strength, stubbornness, and loyalty have inspired us to rush in where fools fear to tread, or even angels, for that matter.

Several years ago, there was talk in our neighborhood of a man who was entertaining young boys too frequently. A mother of one of the boys came to talk to Mom about it, and next thing we knew, Mom took off with her, marched right into the man's house, and retrieved the woman's son. She then called the police. They investigated, and the guy ended up in jail.

When it comes to children, there is no stopping my mother. If she thought someone around us was a bad influence, she was right out there kicking you-know-what and taking names. So would I, now, believe me. It reminds me of what actor Carroll O'Connor said not too long ago: "Get between your kids and harm whenever you can." I grew up in a time that was somewhat wilder than my mom's in her youth, and now it's even worse, which means we all have to be more vigilant. We deal with so many families who have lost their kids that it makes us even more conscious about child safety with each passing day.

As for her own children's safety, Mom can be an avenging angel, even toward other children. I was playing outside one day when I was little when a few boys on bikes came up and almost ran me over. My mom went screaming down the street, and in no time she had all the parents and the boys in the lower half of the block outside. To say she read them the riot act is a cliché as well as an understatement, as she informed them in no uncertain terms what would happen if they ever did hit me, or even thought about it.

She used to say to Paul, Mary, and me, "If you die, I'll kill you," and we'd all laugh. She was always crazed about our going out in the street, running in parking lots, or putting ourselves in any place where drivers might be speeding or just not paying attention. So one day after kindergarten, instead of walking home in my usual direction, I decided to take a shortcut through a parking lot. As I was walking along, I suddenly heard the screech of tires and saw a car coming at me out of the corner of my eye. Being quick and agile, I jumped up on the hood of the car rather than have it hit me (my guide Charlie's intervention). The poor woman driver was so shaken up that she insisted on driving me home. I can't say I was looking forward to that, but she *did* drive me to our apartment. Mom was doing readings in the front room, with three other people waiting in the utility room. Mom opened the door to find me with this total stranger who was trembling like a leaf. The woman explained what happened, and I instantly started crying and screaming, "Mom, please don't kill me!" Imagine what Mom's client and the people waiting in the utility room must have thought. I got "the look" and was sent to my room. Later we had a long talk about . . . etiquette, you might say. What has become a family joke must have sounded like anything but a joke to the other people in the house.

I was in the first grade when I decided that I just didn't want to be in school that day. During the Pledge of Allegiance, I started to wobble around. The teacher stepped over and asked what was wrong. I gravely announced that I was sick. She asked me what I had eaten that morning. I thought for a second and then said, "Nothing." She asked me why, and I said, "Because all the bowls were dirty." Outraged, she grabbed my hand, marched me home, and pounded on the door. Same scenario as before—Mom interrupting a reading to answer the door, more clients waiting in the utility room. My teacher scolded my mother, saying that I was sick from not having eaten because the dishes were dirty. Another "look," and I shuffled off to my room.

That long talk later was about honesty. I argued that the night before, they *had* been dirty, trying to kind of skip over the fact that they had been washed after dinner. What a web we weave.

Poor Mom, poor clients. I never forgot that lesson and never faked being sick again. I'm passing down to my kids that if you tell fibs, then no one will believe you when you tell the truth. And to this day, I have never lied to my mother. In fact, she laughingly says that sometimes I tell her *too* much. I can't blame her. She spends all day with people who want to tell her everything—to confess to her, in a way. But she never throws things up in anyone's face. When it's done, it's done and it's over, thank God.

Following Mom's example as a parent, Gina and I aren't raising Angelia and Willy in a dogmatic environment. We pray, and we send petitions to God, which Angelia loves—she carefully writes hers out and then burns them in the fireplace, as I'm sure Willy will when he's old enough. But we believe much less in ritual and ceremony than in following Christ's example and trying to play an active role in humanity. If they're not careful, people can spend so much time in prayer that they miss out on helping others. That's one thing I never worry about in our family and among our 50 ministers. We are an active, hands-on group, with an online cyber-ministry, prayer chains, a crisis hotline, healings, and countless other services—and with God's constant help, there's not a day that goes by when we aren't focused on making a difference.

CHAPTER TEN

More about My Mom

My mother isn't just a "morning Mom"—she's an "*early-morning Mom*"—a woman who's on the go at the crack of dawn. She's an insatiable reader and usually has three or four books going at once. She isn't moody, and she doesn't seem to have a lot of hormonal fluxes to deal with, which I'm sure helps her cope so well and be so successful in a so-called man's world.

Speaking of men, not only does she gravitate toward them for the majority of her friendships, but they have always flocked to her in abundance. While I was growing up, such dear friends as Dr. Small and Dr. Yarbroff helped fill in as father figures, and before that, I've been told by more than one witness that she received seven marriage proposals in one week. Mary Margaret, her friend of 55 years, once predicted to me that the day Mom passes, she'll still be surrounded by men, because it's been that way since grade school, and it's never stopped.

It's not so easy for a son to think of his mother as anything but Mom, but I have no trouble understanding why men love being around her. She has a dynamite personality and a sense of humor that makes God smile, and she accepts everyone for exactly who they are without ever judging them. I gave her a 60th birthday party and danced the first dance with her, and as I was twirling her around, I said a prayer in my heart that God would give me many more years with this amazing woman who has been such a remarkable mom—while still giving the world a whole new perspective on psychics and spirituality. She belongs to *us* now, but I know that someday she will belong to the ages of greatness, with God's blessing.

There is also a childlike quality in my mom that is irresistible. She doesn't cry often, but when she does, her lip quivers, just like Gina's and Angelia's—enough all by itself to send me racing out for presents and jewelry.

She loves to shop, but rarely for herself. Above all, she loves to go to dinner with friends and talk about everything from philosophy and religion to the latest movies. She loves to travel and lecture. She doesn't have much patience watching TV, unless it's educational—A&E and Discovery are her favorite channels. There are many things she feels passionate about, but none more than children and animals.

She hates camping. We used to do that from time to time when I was growing up, and God bless her, a "camping Sylvia" is not a pretty sight. I remember one outing in particular (our last, I might add) when I was young. It was cold and rainy, admittedly unpleasant, and after giving the trip her best shot, Mom announced to my dad, her first husband, in no uncertain terms, that either we were leaving or she was pouring kerosene on the tent and burning it. You guessed it—we left.

She loves to laugh, and if you ever see her truly break up, you'll see how hysterical and infectious her laughter is. We once timed her during one of those "break-ups," and she laughed for two-and-a-half minutes straight without ever taking a breath.

Mom is fiercely loyal, and once she assigns herself to you, that's it. Her devotion to talk show host Montel Williams, as I mentioned before, is a perfect example. There is no written contract of exclusivity on daytime television between them. There doesn't need to be. No piece of paper in the world is as sacred to Mom as her commitment to her promises, and she doesn't choose the objects of her loyalty lightly. Montel has earned her eternal respect—not only as a result of his uncompromising professionalism, but also by being such a remarkable, compassionate, and active humanitarian, doing more behind the scenes for society than most people even know.

Her friendships, even with her old boyfriends, last forever. She especially loves and supports the Benedictine nuns who taught her in high school. And she has a fascinating relationship with Africa, loving Kenya almost as one loves a lover. All she has to do is speak of it and her eyes glaze over.

What makes her mad? Any person or animal being abused. Telling her she looks tired, or that she's doing too much. And anyone trying to control her life. God knows I've tried. Mom has a vulnerable side, but beneath that is a stubborn woman who wants her own way. People seem to feel that she not only needs protection, but that maybe she got where she is by luck or something. If anyone in this profession happens by some fluke to get somewhere through luck, you can bet they won't stay there. Hurt a loved one or her family and you could have an enemy on your hands—not vengeful, but very quick to tell you when you have gone too far. She believes as I do that no one, herself included, can forgive everything, and at that point you have to just leave the forgiveness to God.

She loves shoes with a passion, but she hates fussing with herself and says she wishes she could just be dipped and then head on out the door. She always cautions against getting caught up in your own press releases, and she doesn't get plugged into her celebrity status. As I mentioned before, but will mention again because it's the last thing people would ever guess about her— Sylvia Browne is very shy. Hard to believe, but the absolute truth.

She doesn't believe in dogma, sin or hell. She believes we're all here to learn on behalf of God. Can she be infuriating? Definitely. Especially when she feels she is right. We have a running joke when we fight—after it's over I always go and ask her if she's sorry. That always makes her laugh, and then she finally says, "Okay. Sorry." Do I say I'm sorry? No. Usually I *am* sorry, but I love to feel that I at least have *some* control.

I'm not as outwardly affectionate as Mom is. I'm not a big hugger or kisser and tend to show my love and devotion in other ways. She says it's because she kissed me so much when I was little that I finally started just squealing with aggravation.

She has not one ounce of prejudice or bigotry, against anyone or anything, no matter what religion, color, creed, or station in life. In the TV and film world, she treats everyone from the stars to the stagehands as the equals she knows they are. She hates judgment and says the only people she judges are those who judge. And none of us hang out with other psychics. It has nothing to do with jealousy or competition. Mom just wonders how, if psychics are busy hanging out together, they could be getting as much done as possible for other people.

I know my mother longs to have more time to write, and also to work with law enforcement and parents of missing children *pro bono*. She'd even like to continue her work on archaeological digs, as she did in Kenya with Dr. Richard Wilding, the National Museum's Director of Coastal Sites and Monuments. She did so at the request of a Kenyan cabinet member named Phillip Leakey, son of the world-famous archaeologists. They went on an exploration of a deserted city called Gedi, which was mysteriously vacated in the 15th century, and Mom told them all sorts of things about the people of Gedi and what happened to them, which they were later able to verify. That experience got into her soul and has never left, and she would love to do more. I wish these things for her more than anything. But she, like me, will never quit serving people, even though it takes so much work and so much money to keep everything going.

My mom will be the first to tell you she doesn't own anything except her furniture and her prized Limoges boxes, icons, thimble collection, and angels. She was into angels long before they came into vogue. Every religion has angels, and it's just now, with the Age of Awakening, that they're coming into their own. Mom and I are both worried about the millennium—not because of Y2K, but because the population has been fed panic in large spoonfuls. The only danger stemming from the turn of the century won't come from outside sources—it will come from people and their terror. If everyone begins hoarding food, water, and guns and there are sudden runs on banks, then we could all be in for a lot of heartache, not to mention potential martial law.

Fear is a dangerous thing, and mob fear is even more ominous. Mom and I are devoting a lot of our time these days, with the millennium upon us, to quelling as many fears as we can, promising everyone who asks and many who don't that January 1, 2000, really will be very much like the day before; and on January 2, we'll all go right back to work just like always.

Even with the world as turbulent as it is, Mom and I believe that by and large, people are basically good. Our commitment to our clients is to help them see more clearly, cope with life's inevitable bumps and bruises, and see the future as it *really* is— not necessarily how they *think* they want it to be, but what their contract reads. As the saying goes, God really does answer prayers, it's just that sometimes He says no.

She has a few close girlfriends—Susan Joseph, Leigh Taylor Young, and last but not least, Lindsay Harrison. Mom did a reading with her and told her they would work together, and they now have two books coming out. There are many more dear friends, but except for FBI agents, doctors, lawyers, and others who started out as professional relationships, the above women are my mom's closest girlfriends. They appreciate the fact that with her schedule there isn't much time to pal around, but when there *is* time, they love doing "girl things" together. She told me the other day that Lindsay bought her a heated eyelash curler, and she was all excited to try it out. It reminded me of Eya with a new dress. If men always stay little boys, there is certainly a little girl in most women, and there is definitely a very dear one inside my mom.

As I touched on earlier, Mom is especially drawn to the people of Kenya and knows she has lived there many times. She feels the same way about Egypt. Not only have she and Gina and I shared past lives, but she and her husband, Larry, have been together in past lives as well. One of the joys of the psychic gift is the knowledge of past-life connections, so my knowledge that I have been with my children before gives me a very sacred awareness of the continuity of life and love.

I would love to convince Mom to exercise more, but she says she gets plenty of exercise running in airports. She used to work out regularly, but the only way to force her to do it is to get her a trainer. When I try to train her myself, it doesn't work—she says I'm too hard a taskmaster. So we leave that issue alone, especially when she takes such delight in pointing out that her mother lived to be 91 years old and never exercised a day in her life.

And let's face it, how can you argue with someone who's at a dead run all the time? One of her bodyguards, Jim, has begged me to convince her to slow down so that he can protect her better. I just stared at him. The poor guy's only 35, for God's sake—he'll learn. She's going to hit the roof when she reads for the first time in this book that Jim is under strict orders to call me after he's safely escorted her back to her hotel while she's on the road. I can hear it now. "So you think I'm a baby, and I can't take care of myself, huh?!" Blah, blah, blah . . . *yes,* Mom!

It's ironic. When I was younger and running around, *she* was worried. Now *she's* running around, and *I* worry. Mom's right—everything goes in cycles.

CHAPTER ELEVEN

Mom's been on the road for two years now, and even though she likes nothing better than live audiences, I know she's wearing down. Her life consists of phone and letter readings every day; crime solving and other *pro bono* work; taking care of her church and staff; lectures; television appearances; and writing books. She also makes time for her other priorities—being a mom, a grandmother, a great friend, a cook, a homemaker, and a wife. When she was in her 30s, five different doctors told her she would burn out if she didn't slow down. The last of those doctors died three years ago.

My life is a little calmer, but not much—20 readings a day; answering questions by mail; *pro bono* work; writing this book; and trying to be a great husband, father, son, and, very often, a cook. I learned from my mother that a life filled with "busy" is a happy life because it's blessed with so much purpose and direction.

And, like Mom, I believe that two of the key ingredients to real health are staying busy and devoting your life to helping people.

The People in Our World

As Sylvia Browne's son, I'm always so proud when people recognize her. But when they begin to push and shove, I admit, she handles it gracefully, while it makes *me* a nervous wreck. When we go to New York every Christmas, a place very dear to her heart because the ambience there is so stimulating, everyone from the cab drivers to the teamsters to the store clerks and bell-hops to just the passersby on the street yell "Hello" to her, usual-ly with a big "thumbs-up" to go along with it, and tell her openly how much they love her. In Los Angeles, they tend to keep a little more respectful distance, but still always smile and say they appreciate her work. In Northern California, they just stroll up and start right in asking questions. In fact, no movie star could have caused more excitement than Mom did one day when she showed up at the DMV to renew her driver's license.

That reminds me of something that makes me chuckle— wherever Mom goes, people say, "I didn't expect to see you here!" She always replies, "Well, I have to be *some*where." Let's face it, she's got a point.

My mother never drops names, but I don't mind doing it every once in a while on her behalf, because she's always so gen-erous in sharing her friends, including the celebrities, with me and the rest of our family. I've seen with my own eyes that she treats everyone exactly the same, too, and doesn't get tongue-tied in any situation. We were at dinner one night with the Stallone family, and she was introduced to Frank Sinatra, Milton Berle, Jack Carter, and Diane Ladd as if it were just another evening out with friends. The aforementioned Leigh Taylor Young and Sally Kirkland are long-time friends, she knows Cindy Williams, and she's very close to Renee Taylor.

Renee, in fact, gave her a big party about 12 years ago that she's never forgotten, where she met such friends of Renee's as George Peppard and Susan Strasberg, as well as many prominent people in her own field—Dr. Melvin Morse, Stanley Krippner, Dr. Thelma Moss, Dr. William Yarbroff, and hundreds more. Mom also still cherishes a great conversation she had with Joe DiMaggio when she did a special about Marilyn Monroe's death.

She adores Ron Ziskin from Four-Point (the production company that produced *The Other Side* and many other of my mother's specials), Ron Lyons, Steve Ober, Robert George at Mary Tyler Moore (MTM) Productions, Phyllis Diller, and Tim Conway, who won $800 at the track when she told him which horse to bet on. She's close to the legendary casting director Marion Dougherty, as well as soap stars and radio personalities such as Art Bell and Kelly & Kline. Her list of friends looks like a *Who's Who*, and yet I've found almost all of them to be sweet, unassuming, very grateful, good sports, and as insecure as the rest of us are who've found ourselves in the public eye. From Kenya to Egypt to England to Argentina to everywhere else in between, you'll find not just acquaintances of Mom's, but true, dear friends.

My mother has a tendency to put the strangest people together at parties and still have it work out perfectly. I once heard someone say, "I wouldn't miss one of Sylvia Browne's parties if I had two broken legs."

One party in particular has become a long-standing family joke. Mom's sister, Sharon, was dating a guy named Bob who Mom thought was a user, and she made no bones about sharing that opinion with Aunt Sharon and Sharon's friends. Shortly before Aunt Sharon and this guy arrived for dinner, Mom shared one more observation about Bob: "Besides, he reminds me of a frog." Moments later, the doorbell rang and there they were, Aunt Sharon and Bob, and as if by some divine hand or equally divine infusion, Bob walked in, looked around the room, and I swear to you, greeted us all with a resounding "Ribbit"! I know. I wouldn't have believed it either if there weren't so many eyewitnesses who still remember that moment to this day. Most of them still aren't convinced it wasn't a planned entrance, but Mom and I both know it wasn't. And incidentally, thank God, Bob finally just hopped away.

Like Grandma, Like Grandchild

Nothing makes Angelia more ecstatic than when Mom comes home from road trips and she gets to reunite with her greatest playmate and mentor. They especially love playing psychic games together—"What's in the closed box?" or "Close your eyes and feel the color I'm holding." Eya always gets them right. Just the other day she was in the office bathroom with Mom (I wonder if poor Mom will ever get even a moment of privacy in the bathroom!), and when they came out, Angelia asked, in front of everyone, "Bagdah, who is that dark-haired woman who's always with you?" Mom nonchalantly told her, "That's Francine, my spirit guide." The whole staff went into a spin. It's amazing how long they have been with us without losing their ability to get overwhelmed when "hits" like that happen. I find that to be so charming—better that than taking everything for granted.

About a week ago, out of Eya's earshot, Mom said to Linda, my secretary, "You'd better get your teeth fixed before they pop out of your mouth." Later, Eya was sitting with Mom, and out of the blue, announced, "Ya-ya (Linda) has bad teeth, Bagdah." Two days later, Linda broke two front teeth and had to have them pulled. Mom and Eya just gave each other a silent, identical "I told you so" look.

By the way, it's not unusual for the staff to sit politely through warnings like that from us and then ignore them completely, which *does* tend to frustrate us sometimes. Pam, who's been with us for 28 years, suggested to Mom, "Maybe if you'd charge us, we'd listen." Sad, but probably true.

Medical Intuition

Mom, Eya, and I all love the medical field. We're not formally trained in that area, but in all of our cases, it seems to have come about as part of our gift. I've wondered if it might be a legacy from my great-great grandmother, who was a psychic and a doctor in Germany quite a feat for a woman in those days. Or, as Mom says, maybe it comes from the spirit doctors on the Other Side who help us through infused knowledge.

Eya assisted Gina's doctor with the ultrasound for Willy and was in the room when he was born. She was so excited, especially by the cord. Besides, she had prayed and prayed for Willy, and finally here he was, "all finished from God."

Mom has an almost spooky ability to do body scans and tell people what their doctors should look for. I'm good at this as well, and I'm finding that every day it's coming in stronger. I'm sure that's why we have so many doctors on referral. We both believe in vitamins and alternative medicine, but we *never* understate the importance of medical doctors. Like Mom says, "You don't treat a hot gall bladder with herbs and a crystal—you get the damned thing taken out!"

Mom and I have both noticed and commented on the fact that we're seeing an increase in depression among our clients, as well as a rise in illnesses we never heard of before in her lifetime or mine, such as fibromyalgia, candida, chronic fatigue syndrome, and strange viruses that no one can diagnose. I'm sure the medical profession is stunned, too.

I'm not a pessimist, but I can't help but wonder if maybe this planet is somehow avenging all the harm we've done to its animals, its rain forests, its water, its atmosphere, and so on. Abuse anything as we've abused this earth, and you can't realistically expect it not to retaliate somehow. Mom and I believe that now is one of the worst eras in this planet's history. It will recover, though, and in the meantime, it says a lot for all of us who were brave enough to come here at this of all times and "graduate" faster for God.

Angelia's love of anything medical extends to everything from shots to Band-aids. One of the few things she loves more is another family passion—animals. I've been surrounded all my life with dogs, cats, bunnies, hamsters, rats, frogs, mice, fish, etc., etc. At one time we raised Rhodesian Ridgebacks, which were originally bred to be lion-hunters in Africa. Simba, one of our beloved females, once gave birth to 13 healthy puppies, with Mom right there helping, straining, and grunting right along with her. People often ask us if animals go to heaven. Of course they do. Heaven wouldn't be heaven without them. They are God's pure creatures—or, as Mom calls them, angels on Earth.

In sharp contrast, we're also asked a lot if evil really does abound in the world. And again, of course it does. But Mom and I both believe that evil is something to be observed and then left alone. You can't convert evil to good. It's interesting that we never get evil people as clients. I'm convinced that they're repelled by the concepts of spirituality and direction.

CHAPTER TWELVE

This may sound strange, but I realized recently that I live my life the way I eat my dinner—one thing at a time. I focus on what's right in front of me at any given time and only move on when I've finished. My mother used to constantly say during dinner, "Chris, come on, try *every*thing." And I'd constantly reply, "I will, when I get to it." Mom, on the other hand, tastes everything right away. Her plate is always full of many projects, all of which get her attention without any of the others being disregarded. And from what I can tell, the more the merrier.

Right now, Mom has audio books to tape. She also happens to be reviewing countless albums and CDs, is looking for meditation music; preparing for a Pay-Per-View appearance; taping more *Montel* shows (her favorite); is in the middle of a lecture tour that doesn't end until the year 2001; is writing two more books; is starting a book with my daughter that will be a child's guide to God; and is keeping up with her schedule of readings and doing *pro bono* work for the medical and law enforcement communities. And then, as I've mentioned, in her spare time (?!) she manages to juggle her roles of wife, mother, friend, and, above all, grandmother. Does it make you as tired reading that as it made me just telling it to you?

We were on an elevator together in her apartment building in L.A. the other day, and a neighbor mentioned that a woman in another apartment had died the day before. "She was very old," the neighbor told us. "At least 62." I couldn't resist poking Mom, and she glared back at me. Seeing Mom at 62, I truly believe her youthful demeanor stems from a combination of genetics and mind-set. All the females on Mom's side of the family have lived into their 90s. But they've also been strong-willed, and it's not in their temperament to indulge themselves when it comes to thoughts of illness, age, or death. Mom told me recently that when she does die, she wants to just be thrown over the back fence. For one thing, she doesn't want any big deal made over it when she goes Home, and for another thing, she can't stand the neighbors.

Mom's biggest concerns are making sure that everyone around her is happy; that she's earning enough money to support her staff, ministers, and church; and that she's never, ever spending too much time away from her grandchildren. She and Eya have a whole lot in common, needless to say, and Willy's disposition make her smile no matter what mood she's in.

I've asked myself a million times what on earth Willy is doing in the middle of such an intense family. The answer always comes through loud and clear: "Bringing simple joy and happiness to a very complicated group of people." He has Mom's and my Humanitarian theme, with the Harmony theme on top of it, and even though he's not even two years old yet, I can already see his themes materializing. If anyone feels sad or upset, Willy runs over and hugs their legs. No matter how much he loves something he's eating (that is, pretty much anything), he'll pause to offer you some. When we show him a picture of his sister, he says, "Purdy." He's definitely the angel of Mom's heart, and of the hearts of everyone who knows him.

I'd love to say he takes after his father, but Mom would never let me get away with it. She loves to tell a story about when I was a year and a half old and bouncing as hard as I could on the couch. She told me several times to cut it out, but I kept right on going. Finally, totally exasperated, she yelled, "Chris, if you don't stop that, you'll have to go to your room." Upon hearing that, I jumped down off the couch, face red, fists clenched, and yelled back, "If you'll fight me, I'll fight you." Apparently it didn't scare her too much, since I still ended up in my room. But she said she walked around for hours after she escorted me there, wondering where on Earth I came from. So I guess it's only fair that a generation later, I wonder the same thing about *my* son.

Mom has always been very smart about how to motivate me. It started in early childhood, when she knew I thought nothing was more boring than shopping for clothes, but she'd get me there by saying, "Who can run the fastest to the store?" I couldn't resist a challenge then, and that's still true to this day. The old reverse-psychology approach "I'll bet you can't . . ." has always worked on me, too, although no one has to challenge me now—I challenge myself enough for all of us, whether it's about body-building, performing, or my readings. "Good" has never been good enough for me. I strive for excellence, and making that a constant self-challenge is a guarantee against letting monotony and mediocrity seep in.

As I write this chapter, I'm in the middle of a horrible case of poison oak, which I'm very allergic to. Angelia got home from a field trip, and I, not thinking, was the one who bundled up her clothes from that day and carried them to the laundry room. That's all it took—she walked through it, and I got it. Swollen, badly inflamed eyes, itching like crazy . . . but miserable as I've been with this, I've smiled more than once remembering my childhood poison oak encounters, followed by Mom and her ever-present calamine lotion, staying up all night with me, challenging me to see how long I could go without scratching, and then imitating me until we were both hysterical. I echo what Art Bell said so lovingly to Mom on his radio show: "Sylvia, if I were sick or dying, you're the one person I'd want with me." She never calls herself a healer, but her wonderful energy gives you the comfort of knowing that everything really will be all right.

There are other definite perks to being her son, besides the obvious. I had some workers at my house who were getting on my nerves because they didn't seem to be getting the job done, and I was constantly monitoring them while trying not to lose my temper. One afternoon when I was about at my wits' end, Mom happened to come by. On her way through the house, she said hello to the workmen and chatted with them for a minute, as she does with everyone. After she left, the head of the crew came to me and said, "Chris, I hope you don't think I'm crazy, but your mom looks just like that psychic woman who's on *Montel* a lot." I was busy writing, so I barely looked up as I told him, "She is. My mom is Sylvia Browne." The next thing I knew, he was war-whooping his way up and down the halls, sharing this news with his crew, shouting about how his wife would never believe this— and you've never seen work get done better and more quickly than it was at my house from that day on.

Mom's celebrity ego is nonexistent. Her "I am" was alive and well long before she became famous, and it will stay that way no matter what. Someone asked her in an interview recently what she would do if it all went away. She said she would go right on loving her life and her family, because "first and foremost, I can always serve God, on a small scale as well as a large one." She's warned me for years against getting caught up in reading press releases and believing you're a big deal just because people have heard of you. Only you and God really know who you are and what your motives are. Besides, as she points out, "It's not about winning popularity contests; you just have to be true to yourself."

The woman you see on television, at lectures, and in readings is exactly the woman we know and love at home. She always says, "You can't fool the camera—it will always find your heart and soul. If I tried to be someone different in public from who I am in private, I'd be a hypocrite."

Can she be quick with a smart-ass remark when the situation demands it? You bet. Can she get short-tempered and aggravated? Absolutely. She can cry as easily as she laughs, and when she's on a full roll, she's almost hard to be around because the atmosphere she creates crackles with energy. On her most recent lecture tour in the South, she came home healthy as a horse, while both her bodyguards and one of the staff members who traveled with her ended up with the flu, and two others were almost immobilized from exhaustion for days. In other words, a 62-year-old woman completely wore out five people with an age range of 35 to 44.

Mom just shakes her head and says it's probably because they didn't eat enough pig hocks and lima beans when they were growing up. Between you and me, I've never quite understood that—it must be a borderline-Southern thing. Mom's very proud of being a Missouri girl, a daughter of the Mason-Dixon Line. I know Missouri is the "Show-Me" state, but there are times when Mom really pushes that envelope. And when she's in full swing, she can be like a drill sergeant—not mean, but with a crystal-clear philosophy of "Just do it!" long before the Nike people ever adopted that as their motto.

Mom is certainly complex. You can never second-guess her. Also, in case you haven't noticed, she'll sometimes get your attention through shock value or just by her willingness to be out-rageous. I've discussed this with her oldest friends, and it definitely isn't something she's developed with age—she was apparently like this in grade school. Her friend Mary Margaret has described my mother on the playground giving mini-readings, and then getting up in front of the class and regaling them with stories that we realized later were actually linked to her past lives.

CHAPTER THIRTEEN

Mom once asked her Grandmother Ada, whom she adored, if she thought Mom would ever be as spiritual as she was. Grandma Ada nodded with absolute certainty. I may be too close to judge, but I'm betting she's more than proved Grandma Ada right.

I was at a lecture recently when a little boy who couldn't have been more than about seven years old came up to the mike and presented Mom with a friendship bracelet, which she adored and immediately put on. He then asked her if anything bad would ever happen to him in his life. Her face literally softened and shone with love as she told him, "Ricky, if anything bad does happen, your angels will bear you up, lest you would dash your feet against the rocks." His smile at that was radiant, and for a moment there wasn't a dry eye in the house.

Notice, by the way, that even though Mom would love to have been able to tell that sweet child that no, nothing bad would ever happen to him, her contract with herself and with God is that she has to tell the truth. I'm the same way.

And so is Angelia, as we were reminded again the other day. It was Larry's (Poppy's) birthday, and the office staff planned a surprise party for him. Eya strolled right in and told him about it but instructed him to act surprised. Mom overheard her, and a little while later, she casually asked Eya how Poppy knew he was having a party. Eya looked up at Mom with those big violet eyes and said, "I told him, Bagdah, because I can't keep a secret."

Mom and Eya are spending the summer together, and I've never seen my daughter so excited. Those two are so connected, literally, that they remind everyone of a kangaroo and her baby—Angelia simply wraps herself around her Bagdah and stays right there. We went on a family cruise to Alaska last year. How many people do you know who've actually lost weight on a cruise? But Mom did. Her secret? "The Angelia Diet." Try eating three meals a day with an adoring five-year-old attached to your lap between you and your plate and see how much of those meals you'll really end up eating.

Not that you'll ever hear a word of complaint from Mom. She shows and expresses her love to her grandchildren just as often and as readily as she did to her own children, and unlike some parents, when she felt she was overly cross with us, she would apologize. I've heard people try to justify not apologizing to their children by claiming that it will undermine their authority. I think that's so wrong. Children need to feel respected, just as adults do, and it's healthy for them to learn that their parents make mistakes, too. Who wants to be around, let alone raised by, a perfect person?

Mom has always said that at the heart of every wrong, you'll find greed, jealousy, and/or vanity. I took issue with her for years about that, thinking she was oversimplifying things. But the longer I live, the more I realize that she's right. So was Grandma Ada, when she told Mom early in her career, "What price fame, if you put your ethics and your soul in jeopardy?"

As grateful as we both are for the size of our clientele, it does frustrate us that neither of us can offer much in the way of instant gratification—Mom's waiting list is about a year long, while mine is six or seven months long. We would change that if we could, believe me, but there's only so much we can do, and every once in a while it actually works out for the best. I love hearing clients say, "Chris, my straits aren't as dire now as they were when I booked the reading, but I still want to get your input on my future."

It's hard sometimes to get people to listen instead of talk. I know it's because they want us to understand, but we have to keep saying, "I'm psychic, and I *do* understand, so please don't lead me." There's so much external and internal noise going on around all of us that I'm convinced we as a society have to be more diligent than ever about becoming more aware, and about being better listeners.

You'll never hear Mom and me claiming to be doctors or psychologists. Dr. William Yarbroff once said to Mom, "You cut to the heart of so many of our patients' problems that it saves us doctors a lot of time." But that's the key—it's a collaboration, the doctors *and* us, not us *instead* of the doctors. A woman came to my office just the other day who, it became quickly apparent, was a paranoid schizophrenic. Rather than let my ego get in the way of trying to deal with something beyond even my best psychic expertise, I immediately referred her to an excellent psychiatrist who I knew could offer her much-needed and long-lasting treatment.

I've heard of some psychics who try to single-handedly take on every problem that walks in the door, from medical to psychiatric, and I can't stress this enough—that's not only dangerous, it's against the law. That's how the great Edgar Cayce got in trouble, in fact—by prescribing medicine for his clients without the appropriate licenses and degrees. If you ever find a psychic offering prescriptions, please do society a favor and report him or her to the authorities!

CHAPTER FOURTEEN

I'm often asked, "How do I find my spirit guide or my past lives or my life themes?" My answer: astral travel. You'll never hear that same answer from my mother, who doesn't really enjoy or participate in astral travel much at all, but I have some very quick meditations that can help you with it if you're patient and willing to keep working on it.

Finding Your Spirit Guide

Relax yourself, and light a green candle to signify healing. Lie down in a comfortable position. Now, slowly continue relaxing yourself from the feet up. When you get to your head and the roots of your hair, breathing deeply and regularly, you're ready. In your mind, take yourself to a seashore. See yourself sitting with your back against a palm tree, feet in the white sand, sun on your face, and demand that out of the shadows your guide will appear, sit down, and talk to you. This is short, but effective.

Discovering Your Past Lives

Relax your body. Concentrate on breathing. Relax your feet, ankles, calves, thighs—all the way up your body. When you are totally relaxed, take yourself back to, say, age 20, or any age you can comfortably remember. Keep going back in your life by ten-year intervals, focusing on specific incidents, no matter how important or trivial. Take yourself all the way back to your conception. Then ask to go back through a tunnel of time into a *valid* past. The tunnel is white, and then you see yourself bathed in purple light. Now, see yourself looking at a map. One place will jump out at you from that map. No matter how far-fetched it sounds, *take your first impression.* Leave the word *imagination* out of this equation—just go with every first impression you get as you begin to ask yourself questions: "Do I feel male or female? Am I young or old? Where do I live? Am I rich or poor? What is my name? Is there anyone with me in this past life whom I know in my present life? What is my life's plan? Did I learn from it? What maladies am I suffering from? How did I die in this past life?"

Ask yourself as many questions as you can think of, and just go with the experience and the answers you get. Make a mental note ahead of time to remember this "journey," and write it down in a journal afterwards. Also, while you're in that past life, ask that any negative cell memories that you may have carried over be dissolved in the white light of the Holy Spirit. Conversely, ask that any positive cell memories from that life be brought forward. And *always* add the codicil that any pain that should be tended to by a physician will *not* be alleviated, so that you can and will be responsible for getting it taken care of.

Astral Projection

This is another light relaxation meditation and often works better at night. Start at the feet again, and work your way meticulously up the body, always surrounding yourself with the white light. Then begin to think to yourself that, by your will, you're leaving your body. Visualize that you're outside and above your body now, and then, leaving your body behind, go to some other room in your house. Walk around the kitchen or the bathroom, noticing every detail, and keep remembering that *it's the will of the soul that creates the experience of astral projection.*

If you do this every night for a week or more, a point may come when you actually start to feel yourself vibrate. That's when many people become afraid. If fear creeps in, simply say, "With the help of God, my guides, and my angels, I will make a fast exit." If you hear a "pop" and feel air rushing, that means you're out.

After several nights of staying comparatively close to your body, you'll start to feel more secure, and then you can extend your astral travel to more distant places. Ask to go to the Other Side. Don't worry, you won't break or sever the Silver Cord and be unable to get back. Ask to go to the Hall of Records, and ask that your guide show you your life themes. You'll be amazed at how much information you can gather while your body lies perfectly still.

But do ask for an easy reentry into your body. And do remember that this astral projection exercise is not to be used as a way to hide or escape from life. It is simply to prove that your soul, which is the full essence of who we are, is able to move into and out of this vehicle we call our bodies.

Let's say for the sake of argument that night after night goes by when you don't manage to go anywhere or see anything. That's okay. From the simple act of relaxing, you're opening up your crown chakra to receive telepathic knowledge directly into your mind, which is known as *infusion*. You're also giving God a chance to speak to you (the *good* listening process we talked about earlier), not to mention just clearing out the cobwebs. I promise, whether you actually astrally project or not, you'll come away from the exercise refreshed and confident that you've done something both physically and spiritually healthy for yourself. I've known people who had no "luck" during the meditation, but later, when they went to sleep, they "dreamed" in perfect detail a past life as an American Indian that we were later able to validate through registries at the Oklahoma City Courthouse.

CHAPTER FIFTEEN

We're a society almost obsessed with our bodies—we're so concerned with eating right, exercising, and buying all types of products that promise to make us more youthful that we often neglect our mental and spiritual development, which is really what rules our lives. It's also my experience that men tend more toward being "quick-fix" entities, while women are more patient, contemplative, and meditative.

Especially in this rushed day and age, it would benefit all of us to follow the women's example and take a few extra minutes to calm and clear our overworked minds. There aren't that many places to go in a crowded world to find solace and comfort, but we can always look to our own sacred temples inside ourselves and listen to God's voice.

Don't get me wrong, I'd be the last person to say there's something bad or wrong about the physical or material world. I'm just talking about the importance of balance. I've been a body builder, after all, and according to Mom, I was so attached to my security blanket—a full-sized blanket from her bed, which must have been pretty awkward to drag around—that I would sit by the clothes dryer on laundry day, holding a private little vigil waiting to be reunited with it. That may be another guy thing, come to think of it. Angelia never had a favorite blanket or toy, but Willy is permanently attached to a velvet pillow with tassels—his father's son. Angelia is much more esoteric and nonmaterial, definitely my mom's granddaughter.

We really are a family of writers. Mom's mother, Celeste, wrote for the *Kansas City Star*. Her treasured psychic grandmother, Ada, wrote stories and poetry for the *Springfield Gazette*, and Ada's brother wrote for the Tulsa newspapers. Mom won countless literary contests in high school and college. Now I'm taking my stab at it.

And then the other day, I was listening to Mom and Eya working on their book. Eya was walking back and forth, talking a mile a minute, and Mom was writing as fast as she could. Eya would say, "Read it back, Bagdah," and Mom would dutifully obey. Eya would listen closely and then nod with a firm, "Good. Now, let's go on." I kept thinking, *How much brain can possibly fit into that little six-year-old head?!* If this isn't proof of other lives, I don't know what is. Parents can certainly take some credit, but the soul comes in with a whole lot more for which we can't take either the credit or the blame.

Angelia is definitely the family problem solver—if you present her with a problem, she'll either come up with a solution instantly or she'll bull-dog it until she's beaten it. I think it's part of the psychic mind, and particularly hers, to see alternative roads that might not be readily apparent to the person she's reading and make it possible to circumnavigate some of the obstacles that are bound to come along. No one can or should avoid every obstacle, but a good psychic can help his or her subjects sidestep many of them while staying fairly well on track—instead of wandering clear out into left field and then having to work even harder to get back to their highest, straightest path again.

Helping people avoid obstacles is the biggest reason why Mom and I, and all responsible psychics, must tell the truth. We're written into our clients' charts for that very reason, I believe. For example, I recently "saw" a client's house catching fire. But I made myself go further and "saw" the source of the flames—I told him there was something very wrong with the wiring in his bathroom. He listened, thank God, had an electrician check it out, and sure enough, he found a hot wire in that wall that was just a disaster waiting to happen. And then, of course, there are the countless warnings Mom has given her clients that have literally saved them from everything from car wrecks to plane crashes.

Many clients have said to me, "I wish I had called you two or three years ago and saved myself all that trouble." I always assure them they weren't supposed to call me until exactly when they did, because there are simply things we're meant to go through without warning so we can learn from them.

When I say that Mom and I have been written into our clients' charts, I mean exactly that. There are no accidents. The warnings, or absence of warnings, were all designed for you, *by* you, before you started this lifetime, whether they come from a psychic, a friend, a stranger, or your guides and angels who often have to work overtime to get your attention.

In my opinion, the reason we seem to be getting more and more warnings these days is to demonstrate that the Age of Prophecy is still alive and well as we approach the 21st century. It did not die in A.D. 300, as some scholars have tried to claim. That would be as silly as saying that somewhere along the line, God quit making artists or actors or engineers or architects. Trying to squelch a belief in prophets has never worked in the long run, and it never will.

Parapsychology was officially declared a science in 1968, but even in today's supposedly enlightened world, there are still people who are convinced that this field originates from the devil. Another thing I've never understood—why in all logic would the devil want to predict anything? Isn't that something far more likely to come from God, in His constant, loving effort to protect us and keep us as safe as possible while we're away from Home?

I've never known anyone more devoted to God and Christ than my mother is, with the possible exception of me, and I get furious when someone even thinks about suggesting otherwise. But as Mom keeps reminding me, not that many psychics even refer to God, so she understands the skeptics and the unfair, untrue accusations that we're doing anyone's work but God's. She's very good at just pushing those things away and writing them off to ignorance. I need to learn to be more tolerant on this subject. Not one of my strong suits.

Mom has far less patience, though, with being told what to say or do. Her position is, "Unless you see a suggestion box, please keep it to yourself." One day the staff put a suggestion box on the office wall as a joke. Just to keep them on the edge of their chairs, she pretended that she didn't notice it. And it worked. Their anxiety grew, and there was constant whispering of, "Did she see it? Is she mad? What is she thinking? Why doesn't she say something?" Finally, after a week of their agonizing, she walked in one morning, pointed to the box, and announced, "I *suggest* you take that down!" Needless to say, there was a sigh of relief, because she made it clear that she *did* think it was funny, but no one has ever tried pulling that little stunt again.

I can't tell you the number of people over the years who have come into Mom's life and felt that they knew what was best for her. She always listens politely and then does exactly what she pleases. How do people think she got where she is? By luck? Especially when, God knows, she's tested every single day on who she is and how she does what she does.

She recently did a live question-and-answer special on the Internet. A man came online, declared himself a "true skeptic" (I've always wondered what an *un*true skeptic is), and almost dared her to tell him something he could believe in. She replied, "I don't know *what* you can believe in, but your top left molar is hurting terribly, and the cartilage in your elbow is damaged." He instantly became proof-positive. In case you've ever been curious about this, yes, it is possible to be speechless on the Internet.

You may have heard Mom on a recent radio show, as I did, being asked for a response to a well-known skeptic who called her a fake. She stated matter-of-factly that while she appreciates that everyone has to earn a living somehow, she's curious about why this particular skeptic always insists on his own isolated segment and refuses to confront her face-to-face. She tried to corner him once on a TV show they were both booked on a few years ago, and he literally ran away from her. Oh, well. It's all in a day's, or a lifetime's, work.

We do hate getting lumped into the pot of magicians and sleight-of-hand artists who are more concerned with physical illusions and actual "tricks" than the truth. I assure you that those are completely separate skills, having nothing to do with psychics and spiritual visionaries.

CHAPTER SIXTEEN

The Show Always Goes On

I'd never seen Mom as nervous as she was about her first Pay-Per-View event. I understood it—she wanted so much to communicate her spiritual message without failing anyone on live TV in the process. The curse of the Humanitarian.

God bless Hay House and Montel for this and everything else they do for her, and as her son, I can also add, God bless her for seeing to it that they get back from her as generously as they give. Part of Mom's personal ethic is that if she wins, everyone wins. She couldn't be a vain, greedy, it's-all-about-me diva if she tried.

And speaking of "God bless Hay House"—when I began writing this book, I naturally thought about structure. But finally, with encouragement from this open-minded publisher, I decided that I could communicate best in the form of a stream-of-consciousness conversation. This is the way we all think and speak, after all, and I'm so full of thoughts and memories and gratitude and God's love that I can't imagine trying to contain them all in some kind of strict, linear order. I really appreciate that Hay House agreed with me and let me do this my way.

Back to the Pay-Per-View, though—I need to clarify that Mom's nervousness is limited to certain events and situations. It has nothing to do with the people she'll be working with and talking to. People *never* make her nervous. I've seen her win over some that Godzilla would have run from. Her philosophy is: "They can't eat you." Her biggest fear is disappointing someone. Put her in the position where she can even imagine that happening and you'll have a woman on your hands who could make PMS or full-blown menopause look like child's play. I kept telling her if she'd simply have fun and be herself and conduct the Pay-Per-View with her own brand of spontaneity and humor, she couldn't miss. Start telling her she has precisely x-amount of time with the live audience, then has to go to the phones at precisely x-o'clock, then has to read from the teleprompter again for exactly x-minutes, and you can almost see her head bobbing up and down in a sea of panic.

I would have given anything if her dad, my beloved grandfather, could have been there to introduce her. That would have put her at ease instantly. He introduced her once at a huge lecture with so much love and pride that we still get choked up when we watch the tape of that night, especially when he says in a father's voice full of tenderness, "Everyone should have a Sylvia in their life."

I'm always far more nervous when Mom's on stage than she is. I sweat and strain and almost have trouble just sitting there, not out of a lack of confidence in her, but because I'm rooting for her so hard. I know it's silly, because nothing throws her when she's in front of an audience. If you've seen her in person, you may have seen her casually stopping in the middle of a lecture to 4,000 people and saying, "Wait, what was I saying? I just lost my train of thought." Not only does the audience not mind when she does that, but it puts them on her side all the more. It's absolutely genuine whenever it happens, but she jokes and says she's just checking to make sure everyone's paying attention.

I've seen her go on stage or on camera fresh from a root canal, with a 103-degree fever, with such a bad case of the flu she can barely talk—you name it. This is another inherited trait I can thank her for, since I'm able to work no matter what's going on with me physically, too. It's like our psychic ability has a life of its own, and we're able to separate it from everything else and not let any other force interfere.

On the day of that first Pay-Per-View special, Mom was more terrified than I've ever seen her. I could tell this was so because she wouldn't sit still, and on the rare occasions when she did, she had a preoccupied look on her face. My mother can't sandbag her feelings with me—I know her too well. I debated whether or not to enter into that dark world of fear she was caught in. It wasn't that I wasn't willing to share it with her, it was just that there's only so much you can say. "It will be all right" is about it, but isn't that much help, even when you mean it as sincerely as I did.

Luckily, when her fear was reaching its peak, I had a dream. Very unusual for this family, since none of us often have prophetic dreams, especially about ourselves or each other. But there she was in my dream, in front of the cameras, having a great time.

The next day I made a point of trying to be nonchalant about it. "Mom," I said, "I had a dream last night that you were on Pay-Per-View and having the time of your life." I knew I had struck a chord, because she immediately looked into my eyes, and the first words out of her mouth were, "Did I look nervous?" I said, "No, but your forehead was sweaty. Pray to God that that's the worst thing that happens." And with that she was silent.

She told me it was keeping all the technical details straight that was making her so frightened. What she didn't tell me, but what I knew was true, was that she was frightened of disappointing anyone, particularly Hay House and Montel. Hay House, who published her biography *Adventures of a Psychic*, was footing the bill. As for Montel, she felt that if she did badly or embarrassed herself—as if that were even possible—it would reflect on him. She did admit to him, "I don't ever want to disappoint you," and he frowned and replied, "Don't even go there."

She did great, of course. But when the show first came on live from New York, I could barely watch it. I was like a cat on the proverbial hot tin roof. I had totally absorbed her nerves at that point, and I was feeling sick and anxious. What a curse in many ways to be so tied to someone, and yet in even more ways, what a blessing. Love really can be a many-splendored or a many-splintered thing.

The kids were watching, too, of course, and when Mom made her entrance, we all screamed. Angelia was so proud, and Willy was upset that he couldn't reach through the big-screen TV and touch his grandma. Our house was like a zoo, with staff and other friends gathered around, and when it was over, we were all jumping around whooping and cheering. Gina and I were both babbling idiots when Mom finally called—we talked so fast she couldn't understand a word we were saying.

Eya, of course, went to school the next day and told everyone that not only was she writing a book, but her picture was on Pay-Per-View. She *does* love the spotlight, but she's never pushy or bratty about it, thank God.

Mom just did a Learning Annex lecture in Kansas City, where she used to be a Catholic schoolteacher, and she was thrilled that 20 out of the 55 members of the third-grade class from her old school showed up. The letters they wrote Mom were a joy, and so heart-warming—all the boys were in love with her, and all the girls wanted to be just like her. All my mom's old boyfriends showed up, too, as well as Sister Mary William, her speech teacher. It was a very special night for her.

Then she was off for Indianapolis and St. Louis before heading back to New York for two more *Montel* shows, a sold-out Learning Annex crowd in Broadway's Beacon Theater, a two-day salon with 20 people, and a day of walk-in clients. Next is Los Angeles, with readings every day and more work on her next book, a quick trip to San Diego for a Learning Annex lecture, and back to Los Angeles for a Learning Annex lecture there. And what I've just described is all in one week in April 1999.

Angelia is meeting Mom in San Diego. She has already

informed us that she will not be home this summer because she's going on tour with Bagdah. Eya did promise, though, that she would stop by once in a while to visit Gina and Willy and me. Gee, thanks! (Does the vision of Auntie Mame come to anyone's mind right about now?)

Mom was asked to do a photo shoot for the centerfold of a new magazine's premiere issue. She said she'd do it on one condition: that Eya could do it with her. The magazine came back with a very enthusiastic "Yes!" What a novel twist—grandmother and granddaughter psychics.

Mom and Eya were so cute and excited. Eya got all dressed up, and Gina had to go out and get her a makeup kit! They arrived at the studio and went directly into the makeup room, where they were fussed over and dressed while the photographers got ready.

The photographers tried to position Eya with her head on Mom's chest, but she wouldn't bend her head. Finally, out of exasperation, Mom whispered, "Eya, what's going on? Put your head down!" Eya looked up at her and said, "What, and ruin my makeup?"

Mom, hot and tired, only half-kidding, through clenched teeth, whispered, "Do it or I'll pinch you." So Eya dutifully put her head on her grandmother's chest . . . all the while pinching Mom on the arm when no one could see her. If they use the shot in which Mom is laughing, now you'll know why.

It excites Mom and me a lot that spirituality is coming more and more into full fruition, despite all the frauds and "wanna-be's" leaping onto the bandwagon for a quick shot at power, control, and as much money as they can trick out of people's pockets. In the long run, we're convinced that the public really is smart enough to discern who's authentic and who's faking their way through with a few ringers in the audience.

Whether it's on TV or at a lecture, Mom refuses to hear any of the stories or cases she'll be dealing with before showtime. And you'll notice she never asks yes-or-no questions—those are a device that mentalists use, sometimes very effectively. They go something like this: "I see an older man with you. Could this be your father?" If the subject says yes, the audience is impressed, thinking they're watching a real psychic display in action. If the subject says no, the phony keeps on fishing—"Your grandfather? An older brother? An uncle?" Sooner or later the subject is bound to say yes, and the more gullible members of the audience applaud like crazy. I've learned from Mom never to go on those fishing expeditions, but to commit to your information during the question—"Who is the short older male with a moustache, a scar above his eyebrow, full lips, and a thick build?" The specifics shouldn't come from you when you're with a psychic—they should come from the psychics themselves.

We went to Cabo San Lucas for four days earlier this month before Mom started all this, and it was so good for her. She'd also scheduled a quick vacation right before the Pay-Per-View, but this one was for the kids. I have an amazing shot of her and Willy from the day we spent on a private boat—she was telling him about pirates, and he was staring into her eyes and then scanning the water, apparently looking out for marauding ships. The next thing I knew, the two of them were sound asleep together. Another keeper. Willy can be wide awake, wound up, upset, cranky, you name it, and all Mom has to do is hold him against her ample bosom and sing. Within seconds, his eyes roll back in his head and he's gone, out like a light. He fell off the fireplace while Mom was on this latest trip to New York and bashed his lit-tle nose. We called Mom and put him on the phone with her. The minute he heard her voice telling him it was okay, he knew it real-ly *was* okay, and he immediately stopped crying.

At times like that, it comes back to me as a sick thud in my stomach that Mom went through raising her children alone—two wild boys, loud and rough and ornery, up all night, dashing to emergency rooms and PTA meetings—with her full-time job and anything and everything else Paul and I got ourselves into, and she managed it all with no partner to lean on like Gina and I each have. I guess she's right—whatever doesn't kill you just makes you stronger.

Anything involving children, especially abused or abandoned or missing children, makes us both crazy. They're the one thing that can disrupt our schedule of readings, the true emergencies we'll drop everything to deal with. And no matter how many cases we deal with, all the blood drains right out of us when another of those particular cries for help comes in.

I did a very foolish thing not long ago and incurred my moth-er's wrath. She and Eya have been wanting a Volkswagen Bug to share. Mom has been saving for it—the one thing she'll ever own. I wanted one, too, and I guess to show off, trotted out and bought one. When I told her, she just screamed and refused to talk to me for two days. Looking back, I understand why she was angry, and I really was sorry. I apologized, but she just said, "Uh-huh," and went on talking about something else.

I'll still hear about it, though. She doesn't really hold grudges, but she *never* forgets. Her memory is a file cabinet stuffed full of year, month, time, and date. She also works con-stantly out of both sides of her brain and has ears like a bat. She can hear a gnat flying past at 500 paces. Her sister tells the story of when they were doing postgraduate work in college. A profes-sor was lecturing, while Mom quietly carried on a conversation with Aunt Sharon. In the middle of the conversation, Mom suddenly stopped, raised her hand, answered a question from the professor, and went right back to her conversation with my aunt. I'm sure I've inherited some of that from her and my other psychic ancestors—we can all be worried or depressed or anxious, but the other side of our brain is still able to operate independently and let our psychic abilities flow without interference.

When I look back on our amazing lineage, I'm filled with such a sense of pride and security, and also a lot of sympathy for what they must have gone through. The ones who preceded my mom's grandmother were probably lucky not to have been burned at the stake. I'm sure it helped that along with our psychic ancestry comes an ancestry of deep spirituality about Christ, the Holy Spirit, and God. But considering the judgmentalism about us that I still see and gape at to this day, I can only imagine the scorn our predecessors had to tolerate.

In fact, a man approached Mom in Cabo and said, "So, you're a psychic?" She said, "Yes, I am." He said, "How do you reconcile that with being a Christian?" Without missing a beat, Mom said, "You're a builder, right?" He nodded, without even seeming to wonder how she knew. She asked, "Did God make you what you are?" He nodded again, upon which she smiled and simply added, "Well, God made me what I am, too." He had no response, but I'm sure she gave him a lot of food for thought.

I think it's a case of people just not knowing enough and reading enough about what we do, or realizing that prophets and spiritual teachers have been around forever. Hopefully Mom and I are helping set the stage for Angelia and paving an easier road for her. It's so ironic to me that so many of the early Christians who spoke messages of love, peace, and tolerance were put to death for it.

We even had second thoughts about including the word *psychic* in the subtitle of this book, because it gets misinterpreted as negativity so often, thanks to psychic hotlines and scam artists who are flourishing in the highly publicized anxiety over the new millennium. There probably are some perfectly valid psychics working out there as well—I just don't understand why they allow themselves to be connected to something that looks like a shady, tawdry quick fix.

When Mom was first starting her psychic work, she would go to people's homes to do readings and trances. She says she often felt like the newest barbecue pit on the block. To raise money for her foundation and other humanitarian work, she and her staff would sell dog food, and have spaghetti dinners and rummage sales and car washes—anything to add a few dollars to the cause. I would love to believe I would have had the stamina and commitment to do what she did, but I probably wouldn't have. I'm also not a big fan of rejection, although I do find that the more my spirituality grows, the more courage I have to face adversity.

CHAPTER SEVENTEEN

Mom always says she doesn't know where the years go, and as I get older, I see exactly what she means. It seems like just yesterday she was officiating at Gina's and my wedding, and today Eya is almost seven and William is going on two. The days fly by, and I try to keep track of it and embrace it all, but I'm sure you feel as I do sometimes—that we're all trying to catch a feather in a windstorm.

It also doesn't seem that long ago when Paul and I were children and we were living next door to my Grandfather Bill, Grandmother Celeste, and Mom's sister, Sharon. I didn't realize it at the time, but that was very hard for my mom. She loved her father and was grateful to Aunt Sharon for watching us while she was at work, but her mother was horribly nosy and controlling. In fact, occasionally when people came to visit, Celeste would think nothing of lying and telling them Mom wasn't home.

No matter how busy or broke she was, Mom always made sure there was time set aside for us as a family. She'd take us to drive-in movies once a week or spend evenings with us just popping popcorn and watching TV together. We also loved going shopping with Grandpa, who was great about helping Paul and me pick out clothes. But Mom was still a Catholic schoolteacher in those days and hardly making piles of cash. In fact, she somehow provided gas, groceries, lunch money, and a few clothes on $15 a week. Even in the late '60's, that wasn't much money.

It's funny how it's the little, silly things you remember and cherish, and how it's those things that keep you most alive and your sense of humor at its sharpest. For example, while Mom never really lies, I haven't forgotten how she used to try pawning calf liver off on me as steak. When I finally caught on and confronted her about it, she didn't bat an eye or back down. She just said, "Well, it's *liver* steak."

I also remember my night terrors, and her getting rid of them by talking to me while I slept, and I hope you'll try the same thing with your young children when they're troubled by nightmares, night terrors, or even illnesses—all of which might be a carryover from a past life. Don't worry about keeping your vocabulary too limited and simple for your kids. There are very advanced souls in those little bodies, and they'll always respond to the truth. Mom and I do this for Angelia and Willy, just as Mom did it for me, and her grandmother did it for her:

Wait until the children are asleep, then go sit with them and tell them quietly that if they are carrying over any negativity and pain from a past life, let them be resolved and absorbed in the white light of the Holy Spirit.

You can do this at any age, and with yourself as well. It doesn't just cure nightmares and some illnesses, it also puts the soul in its proper time frame—the *now*.

From the day I was born into this life, I've known without even having to be psychic how loyal Mom is, and almost protective to a fault. She'll instantly spot and react to a sarcastic or unkind remark, and you don't even want to think about demeaning someone in public in her presence unless you want the wreck of the Hesperus on your hands or head. On a recent episode of *Montel,* during the commercial break, a publicist from a publishing company corrected Montel for switching two words in the title of Mom's book as he raved about it to the audience. At dinner that night, Mom informed that publicist in no uncertain terms that never in this life would she ever do that again, especially when Montel was so generously and voluntarily promoting a book he didn't have to say anything about at all if he didn't want to. Correcting Montel, or anyone who's helping you, particularly in front of an audience, was just a huge, ungrateful, unacceptable *faux pas* as far as Mom is concerned, and I promise you'll regret it if you do it within her earshot. I've warned people more than once—don't go after anyone Mom loves unless you want a mother hen on your back, pecking you to death. And I really shudder to think what will happen if Mom ever gets wind of someone being critical of or disrespectful to Angelia!

I remember when my brother, Paul, was in the second grade and my mom, who was also still teaching, went to his annual teachers' conference. Mom thought Paul had been awfully jumpy for the past couple of weeks, and she wanted to know if any explanation for it could be found in his classroom. Paul's teacher began reviewing his grades and homework, and the conversation eventually eased into this teacher's method of disciplining her students. Mom, already smelling a rat, expressed seemingly innocent interest in hearing all about it. So the teacher proceeded to inform Mom that if Paul or any of the other children misbehaved, she simply stood them up in front of the room with a dunce cap on their head so everyone could make fun of them.

"It really works," she said. Mom rose to her feet, said, "So do thumbscrews, but we don't use those, do we?" and marched the teacher straight to the principal's office. She told him what this teacher had been doing and assured him that if it ever happened again—to her own child or anyone else's—she would find a way to own that school so she could fire the whole staff and bring in some good teachers for a change. The principal stammered that he had no idea this was going on, but that just infuriated her even more, and she went on to tear him apart for not knowing.

She also tells the story of seeing a lay teacher at St. Martin's slap a child as hard as she could outside her classroom when she didn't know Mom was watching. Mom successfully had that teacher fired. And this, mind you, was in the days when teachers had a fairly free reign and no one talked about child abuse. Mom believes, and I agree wholeheartedly, that you raise healthy children with love, praise, pride, and firm yet attentive mutual respect—both in the home and at school.

Mom's Childhood

Remembering your past is like looking into a kaleidoscope full of colors and images. Children don't remember their own parents' youth, of course, but if they're smart, they'll listen closely to their parents' stories. I love to hear Mom talk about what she's been through in her lifetime and how she's handled the best and the worst of it—it gives me a richer flavor of my genes, my environment, and the fascinating similarities and differences between us. To understand our parents is to often gain greater insights into ourselves and especially our children, who often seem to manifest the strongest echoes of their grandparents.

All the stories I've heard about Mom's childhood from family and long-time friends indicate that she was as fearless then as she is now, even when life was painful and scary beyond even a psychic child's understanding. Her father, by his own admission, was quite a ladies' man and had many affairs throughout his marriage to her mother. When Mom was three years old, he was dating a cocktail waitress he'd been warned to avoid. One day Mom was playing in the front yard of their house, wearing a yellow dress with a little embroidered boat on it, when a black car pulled to a stop at the curb. A man got out, walked up to this three-year-old child, and said, "Tell your dad if he doesn't leave my wife alone, I'm going to take you away."

On the very rare occasions when Mom and I talk about that incident, she gets a very far-off look in her eyes and says, "That was a bad time, but I kept my eyes down, looking at that little boat and wished with all my might that it would sail me away."

Apparently the man was serious about his rage but decided to be more precise about the target of his threat. Shortly after that, Mom and her mother came home to find Grandpa lying on the floor with a gash on his head. Mom remembers holding Grandma's hand while she cried.

Despite his infidelities, Mom loved her father very much and always understood what a nightmare it was for him, and for all of them, to be with Celeste. Mom protected her little sister from Celeste's manic rages while always basking in her father's love.

Grandma Ada, my mother's adored grandmother, was convinced that Mom could be another Shirley Temple, so off they went to dance and drama classes. At Mom's first recital, she was supposed to come tapping on stage with a little umbrella and dance to "Singing in the Rain." According to Grandpa, moments before Mom's entrance, there was a loud commotion backstage, and he leaned over to Celeste and whispered, "Oh, God, I'll bet it's Sylvia." Sure enough, the door to the stage entrance had stuck only partway open, and Mom, in her frenzy to make her entrance on cue, pulled the open umbrella through the small opening as hard as she could. So the audience was treated to the backstage noise, followed momentarily by the appearance of little Sylvia, holding her broken, inside-out umbrella as if it were meant to look exactly like that.

As the story goes, Mom was completely unflustered and never missed a beat. She just nodded to the pianist and launched into her performance, singing and dancing her heart out. The entertainer in her was born that day, as, was her insistence that the show must indeed go on. She still remembers looking out at this sea of smiles and hearing the delighted laughter mixing with the piano accompaniment, and thinking, *So this makes people happy*. Give a Humanitarian an early clue like that about what makes people happy, and you've given their soul an elixir that will last a lifetime.

Mom had an uncle whom everyone called "Brother." He had cerebral palsy, along with a brilliant mind and a sweet disposition, and my mother adored him and was very protective of him, walking proudly down the street with him from the time she was a small child and just daring anyone to snicker at him. When she was about four years old, the family happened to be living next door to a woman who was insane. Mom and Brother were sitting under an apple tree in the front yard when suddenly, somehow the crazy woman next door broke away from her two nurses and started for Mom. As frail and challenged as Brother was, he managed to get between Mom and the woman, backed Mom toward the house, and took the full brunt of the woman's wrath himself, scratches, bruises and all, until she was restrained. For the rest of his life, Mom called Brother "my hero," and he would beam and swell with pride.

Brother, she says, was a pure innocent, and his two passions besides his niece were news and band concerts. They'd go every summer—Brother, Grandma Ada, Celeste, and Mom—and everyone would encourage Mom to dance. So Mom would go twirling and dancing up and down the aisles while the band played on, stealing a lot of shows and a lot of hearts in the process, I'm sure.

Grandpa also loved telling the story of a weekly post-Depression tradition in which the neighborhood grocer would hold a drawing for a free basket of groceries. Mom, being the cutest and most precocious child in the neighborhood, was given the prestigious job of pulling the winning ticket out of the large drum. Week number one, whose ticket did she pull out but Grandma Ada's. "Coincidence," they all said, chuckling. But after the third week in a row of Grandma Ada's being the winning ticket, the grocer chose another child to replace Mom at the big revolving drum. The first time I heard this story, I asked Mom what was going on during those drawings. She said she would just look at Grandma Ada in the eager crowd, smile and wink at her, and the next thing she knew, her little psychic hand just guided itself straight to her grandmother's ticket. And she was still too young and too innocent to know there was anything wrong with it.

Although she rarely talks about it because she can't tolerate being pitied or even felt sorry for and *never* considers herself a victim, Mom did suffer childhood abuse at the hands of her mother. My grandfather, for example, once left home for three weeks to go to California with a doctor friend in hopes of finding more lucrative job opportunities. While he was gone, Celeste, insanely blaming Mom for his absence, put her in the bathtub and turned on the hot water, full blast, scalding her foot so badly that the skin peeled off all her toes. Mom still remembers standing on one foot, screaming, while Celeste yelled, "Your father went away because you're bad!" A family meeting was hastily convened to mutter about Celeste's mental condition, but in those days, of course, no one quite knew how to talk about child abuse, let alone what to do about it. It was obviously discussed with Grandpa when he got back, though, because he never, ever took off like that again.

To the best of my knowledge, Mom's first headline appeared in the *Kansas City Star* when she was five years old. She and a friend were all decked out for Halloween in little paper costumes, and Mom's friend got too near the open-grated fireplace and promptly began smoldering. Mom grabbed a rug, rolled the child up in it, and saved her life. The newspaper headline read, "Kansas City's Youngest Halloween Hero." A portent of a public Humanitarian life if I ever heard one.

Mom has always assured all of us that our angels really do watch over us, and that no matter how bad things get, God always comes through in the end. When she was six years old, she was riding her bike down the street one day when a young Army recruit in his late teens stopped her in front of his house and said, "Little girl, why don't you come upstairs and take a bath with me?" She cheerfully replied—thank God—"Okay, but first I have to ask my mom and dad." She took off before the boy could stop her, ran in the house and up to her father, who was reading the paper, and repeated the invitation she'd just received. She barely got the whole thing out of her mouth before Grandpa bolted up, sprinted out the door and up the street, and beat that young recruit senseless. She didn't even understand the implication of the boy's suggestion, or her father's reaction to it, until years later, so it really did take a lot of help and luck from God that day to keep Mom from becoming a tragic childhood statistic.

Around that same time, even though he'd stopped traveling, my grandfather wasn't home all that often, and Mom's little friends started asking her why they never saw her daddy. Finally, her flair for the dramatic took over, and one day she replied, "He was killed in a fire." This, of course, created quite a flurry of sympathy and attention, and the more sympathy and attention she got, the bigger the story grew, until it included something about

Grandpa dying in this imaginary fire saving a little girl.

It was close to Christmas, and one day she and Grandma Ada were alone in the apartment when the doorbell rang. There stood a whole group of neighbors with baskets of food and clothing and heartfelt sympathy about the tragic demise of Mom's dad. Mom was hiding behind the door, trying to get smaller and smaller with each condolence, until Grandma Ada calmly pulled her into view and put her through the penitent agony of confessing the truth. Mom still says it was the best lesson she could have learned, not only about how many people a lie can affect, but also of how hollow and insidious lies are because they always come back to slap you in the face. To this day, she won't lie, even if it would save her in some way.

There were ways in which Mom lost out on some of her childhood, as far as I'm concerned, even though it was at her own insistence—she essentially raised her little sister, protected her and ran interference between Sharon and their very difficult mother, Celeste. In other words, her seemingly conflicting themes of Humanitarian and Loner started showing themselves at a very early age. The Loner part may seem confusing at first to those who watch how constantly she's surrounded by people, but I've come to understand that it never, ever means "lonely," or even alone all that often. What it does mean is that throughout her life, while never backing down on her commitment to help everyone else, Mom has had to face most of her toughest and scariest times all by herself. She and I both know how she managed to keep up her strength and her impeccable ethics and her grace under fire, though. No matter how much of a shambles her personal life became from time to time, her spiritual life was, is, and always will be as strong, unwavering, and infinite as her heart.

EPILOGUE

If you'll forgive a little emotionalism, or even out-and-out corniness, I want to close with a personal note to my mother, Sylvia Celeste Browne:

> *I truly am proud of you—not just because of who you are or what you have made of yourself, but also because you're my mom. You've had a huge historical impact on the spirituality of this world, and you've taught me and countless others what it truly means to love God. I've said it before, and it bears repeating—one of the smartest moves I made on the Other Side before I came here was to choose to come down and be with you.*

> Your son, Chris Dufresne

ABOUT THE AUTHOR

Christopher Dufresne is a native Californian, born on February 19, 1966, and he has made his home in the San Francisco Bay Area all that time. He married Gina in 1989, and together they have two extra-cute children, Angelia and William. Since the age of 16, Chris has worked alongside his mother in the family business doing psychic counseling. Although he prefers to remain in the background of the business, he has made several media appearances, notably the *Montel Williams Show, Unsolved Mysteries,* and *People* magazine. His very busy professional life is balanced by spending all his free time with his children; or traveling with his mother to explore other cultures and religions and to expose his kids to the wonderful diversity of our world. Christopher's long-term goal is to be a grandfather and have the joy of showing those precious souls the wonders within God's creation. To contact Chris:

Christopher Dufresne, Sylvia Browne Corp.
35 Dillon Ave., Campbell, CA 95008-3001
(408) 379-7070 • www.sylvia.org

Warning: Neither Christopher nor Sylvia do any business via a "900" hotline service. Any such claim to the contrary is fraudulent. You will never get the real Chris or Sylvia by calling any type of hotline.

We hope you enjoyed this Hay House book.
If you would like to receive a free catalog featuring
additional Hay House books and products, or if you would like
information about the Hay Foundation, please contact:

Hay House, Inc.
P.O. Box 5100
Carlsbad, CA 92018-5100

(760) 431-7695 or **(800) 654-5126**
(760) 431-6948 (fax) or **(800) 650-5115 (fax)**

Please visit the Hay House Website at: **www.hayhouse.com**

Exclusive
SYLVIA BROWNE
Lecture Tape—FREE!

With one-year subscription